FIRST 50 SONGS

YOU SHOULD PLAY ON ACOUSTIC GUITAR

2 About a Girl ..... Nirvana
4 Against the Wind ..... Bob Seger
6 Barely Breathing ..... Duncan Sheik
8 Boulevard of Broken Dreams ..... Green Day
10 Breaking the Girl ..... Red Hot Chili Peppers
12 Bye Bye Love ..... The Everly Brothers
14 Champagne Supernova ..... Oasis
16 Crazy Little Thing Called Love ..... Queen
18 Daughters ..... John Mayer
20 Every Rose Has Its Thorn ..... Poison
22 Falling Slowly .. Glen Hansard and Marketa Irglova
24 Fast Car ..... Tracy Chapman
26 Free Fallin' ..... Tom Petty
28 Have You Ever Seen the Rain? ..... Creedence Clearwater Revival
30 Hey There Delilah ..... Plain White T's
32 Ho Hey ..... The Lumineers
34 A Horse with No Name ..... America
36 I Won't Give Up ..... Jason Mraz
38 Into the Mystic ..... Van Morrison
40 Layla ..... Eric Clapton
42 Let Her Go ..... Passenger
44 Malagueña ..... Roy Clark
46 Me and Julio Down by the Schoolyard ..... Simon & Garfunkel
48 Mean ..... Taylor Swift
50 Melissa ..... The Allman Brothers Band
52 More Than a Feeling ..... Boston
54 More Than Words ..... Extreme
56 Nothing Else Matters ..... Metallica
58 One U2
60 Patience ..... Guns N' Roses
62 Peaceful Easy Feeling ..... The Eagles
64 Redemption Song ..... Bob Marley
66 Ring of Fire ..... Johnny Cash
68 Run Around ..... Blues Traveler
70 Signs ..... Tesla
72 Silent Lucidity ..... Queensryche
74 [illegible] ..... Led Zeppelin
76 [illegible]ds ..... John Denver
78 [illegible] ..... Bob Dylan
80 [illegible] ..... The Eagles
82 Trouble ..... Ray LaMontagne
84 Truckin' ..... Grateful Dead
86 Wagon Wheel ..... Darius Rucker
88 Wake Up Little Susie ..... The Everly Brothers
90 We Can Work It Out ..... The Beatles
92 What I Got ..... Sublime
94 Wild World ..... Cat Stevens
96 Wish You Were Here ..... Pink Floyd
98 Yellow ..... Coldplay
100 Yesterday ..... The Beatles
102 RHYTHM TAB LEGEND

T0079536

ISBN 978-1-4803-9812-2

HAL•LEONARD® CORPORATION

7777 W. Bluemound Rd. P.O. Box 13819 Milwaukee, WI 53213

For all works contained herein:
Unauthorized copying, arranging, adapting, recording, Internet posting, public performance, or other distribution of the printed music in this publication is an infringement of copyright. Infringers are liable under the law.

Visit Hal Leonard Online at
www.halleonard.com

About a Girl

Words and Music by Kurt Cobain

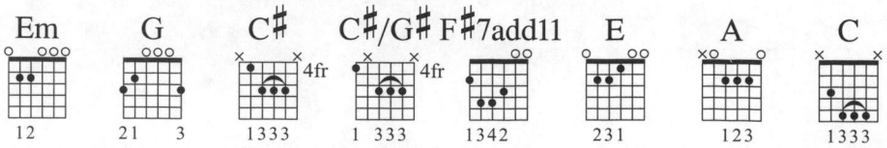

Tune down 1/2 step:
(low to high) E♭-A♭-D♭-G♭-B♭-E♭

Key of Em

Intro

Moderately

Em G Em G Em G Em G

etc.

Verse

Em G Em G Em G

1., 3. I need an eas - y friend, I do, with a
2. I'm stand - ing in your line. I do hope you

Em G Em G Em G

hand to lend. I do think you fit this shoe, I
have the time. I do pick a num - ber too, I

Em G Em G

do, won't you have a clue?
do keep a date with you.

Chorus

C♯ C♯/G♯ F♯7add11 C♯ C♯/G♯

I'll take ad - van - tage while you hang me

3rd time, To Coda

F♯7add11 E A C

out to dry, but I can't see you ev - 'ry night.

Em G Em G Em G Em G

Free. I do.

Copyright © 1989 The End Of Music and Primary Wave Tunes
All Rights Administered by BMG Rights Management (US) LLC
All Rights Reserved Used by Permission

Guitar Solo

Em G Em G

Play 4 times

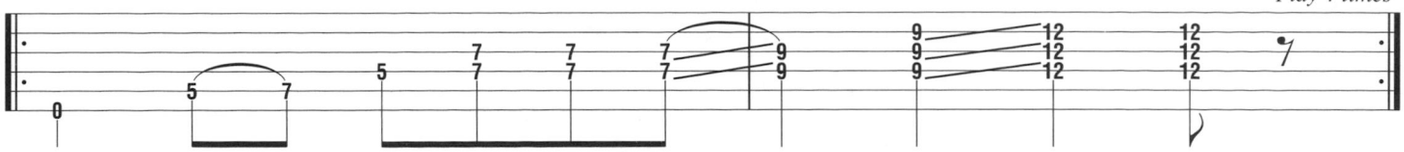

|: C♯ C♯/G♯ | F♯7add11 :| E | A C ||

Interlude ***D.S. al Coda***

| Em G | Em G | Em G | Em G ||

Coda

A C E A C

| ev - 'ry night. No, | I can't see you | ev - 'ry night. |

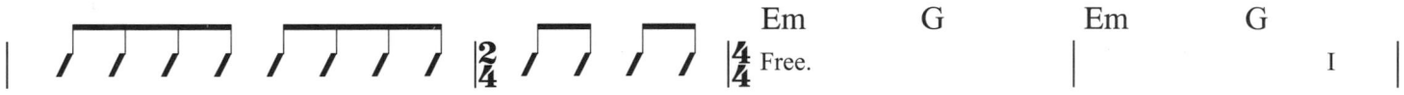

Em G Em G

Free. I

Em G Em G Em G Em G

do. I do. I

Em G Em G Em

grad. slower

do. I do.

Against the Wind

Words and Music by Bob Seger

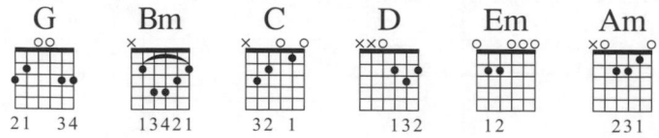

Key of G
Intro
Moderately

Verse

G Bm

1. It seems like yes - ter - day, but it was long a - go.
2. And the years rolled slow - ly past, and I found my - self a - lone.
3. *Instrumental solo*

C G

Ja - ney was love - ly, she was the queen of my nights there in the dark - ness with the ra - di - o play-ing low. And, and the se - crets that we shared,
Sur-round-ed by stran-gers I thought were my friends, I found my-self fur - ther and fur - ther from my home. And I guess I lost my way;

D C G Bm

the moun-tains that we moved there were oh, so man - y roads. I was caught like a wild-fire out of con - trol till there was noth-ing left to burn and noth-ing left to liv - ing to run and run-ning to live, nev - er wor - ried a - bout pay-ing or e - ven how much I owed.

C G C D

Pre-Chorus

Em D

And I re - mem - ber what she said to
Mov - ing eight miles a min - ute for months at a
Solo ends Well, those drif - ter's days are past me prove.

Copyright © 1980 Gear Publishing Co.
All Rights Reserved Used by Permission

G Em C G

me, how she swore | that it nev - er would end. | I re -
time, break - ing all | of the rules that would bend,
now. I've got so much more to think a - bout,

Em D C

mem - ber how she held me oh, | so tight. | Wish I did - n't know now what I
I be - gan to find my - self search | - ing, | search - ing for shel - ter a - gain
dead - lines and com - mit - ments, what to leave in,

Chorus

D G Bm

did - n't know then. || A - gainst the wind, | |
and a - gain a - gainst the wind, |
what to leave out. A - gainst the wind,

C G C

we were run - nin' a - gainst the | wind. We were | young and strong,
lit - tle some - thing a - gainst the | wind. I | found my - self seek - ing
I'm still run - nin' a - gainst the wind. I'm old - er now but still

3rd time, To Coda ***2nd time, D.S. al Coda***

Am C G

run - nin' a - gainst the | wind. | | | :||
shel - ter a - gainst the | wind.
run - nin' a - gainst the wind.

Coda

C Bm D

Well, I'm old | - er now and still | run - nin' | a - gainst the |

C G

wind. | (A - gainst the | wind.) | (A - gainst the ||

Outro ***Repeat and fade***

w/ Lead Voc. ad lib.

C G

||: wind, | a - gainst the | wind.) | (A - gainst the :||

Barely Breathing

Words and Music by Duncan Sheik

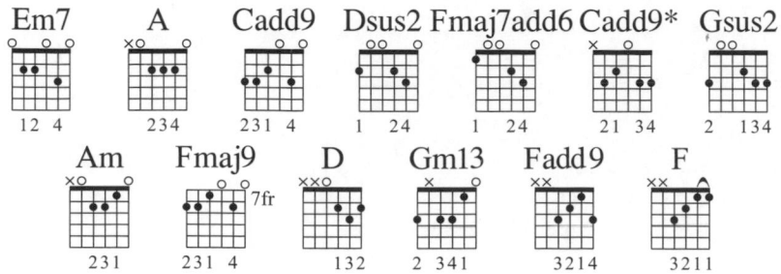

Key of Em

Intro

Moderately slow

Em7 A Cadd9 Dsus2

etc.

1.

2.

Dsus2

Verse

Em7 A

1. I know what you're do - ing, I see it all too clear. I on - ly taste the sa-

Cadd9 Dsus2 Em7

- line when I kiss a - way your tears. You real - ly had me go - ing, wish - ing on a

A Cadd9 Dsus2

star. But the black holes that sur - round you are heav - i - er by far. 2. I be - lieved in your con-fu-

Verse

Em7 A Cadd9

- sion, you were so com-plete - ly torn. Well it must have been that yes - ter - day was the day that I was
- ing, "What's it all a - bout?" I used to be so cer - tain. Now I can't fig - ure

Dsus2 Em7 A

born. There's not much to ex-am - ine, there's noth - ing left to hide. You real - ly can't be se-
out. What is this at-trac - tion? I on - ly feel the pain. Noth - ing left to rea-

Cadd9 Dsus2 Fmaj7add6

- ri - ous if you have to ask me why. I say good - bye.
- son, and on - ly you to blame. Will it ev - er change?

𝄋 Chorus

Cadd9* Gsus2

'Cause I am bare - ly breath - ing, and I can't find the air. Don't know who I'm

Copyright © 1996 by Universal Music - Careers, Duncan Sheik Songs and Happ-Dog Music
All Rights Administered by Universal Music - Careers
International Copyright Secured All Rights Reserved

Am | Fmaj9 | Cadd9*

kid-ding, i - mag - in - ing you | care. And I could stand here | wait-ing, a fool for an-oth-er day.

Gsus2 | Am | Fmaj9

But I don't sup-pose it's | worth the price, it's worth the price, the | price that I would pay, yeah, yeah,

1. | 2.

Cadd9*

yeah. | | 3. And ev-'ry-one keeps ask-: | yeah. But I'm think-ing it

Gsus2 | Am | Fmaj9

o - ver an - y - way. | | I'm think-ing it

Cadd9* | Gsus2 | Am

o - ver an - y - way, | yeah, yeah, yeah. | Oh.

Fmaj9 *To Coda*

Bridge

D | Am | Cadd9* | Gm13

I've come to find | I may nev-er know | your chang-ing mind. | Is it friend or foe?
I rise a-bove | or sink be-low | with ev - 'ry time | you come and go.

Fadd9 F

D.S. al Coda
(take 2nd ending)

Please don't | come and go. | | 'Cause I am bare-ly

Coda

I know what you're do-ing. | I see it all | too clear.

Boulevard of Broken Dreams

Words by Billie Joe
Music by Green Day

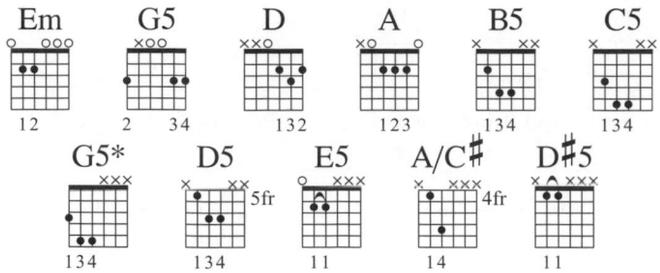

Capo I

Key of Fm (Capo Key of Em)

Verse

Moderately slow

Em G5 D A

etc.

1. I walk a lone - ly road, the on - ly one that I have ev - er
2. I'm walk - ing down the line that di - vides me some - where in my

Em G5 D A

known. Don't know where it goes, but it's home to me and I walk a -
mind. On the bor - der - line of the edge and where I walk a -

Em G5 D A

lone.
lone.

Em G5 D A

I walk this emp - ty street on the bou - le - vard of bro - ken
Read be - tween the lines of what's fucked up and ev - 'ry - thing's al -

Em G5 D A Em G5

dreams, where the cit - y sleeps and I'm the on - ly one and I walk a - lone.
right. Check my vi - tal signs and know I'm still a - live and I walk a - lone.

D A Em G5 D A B5

I walk a - lone, I walk a - lone. I walk a - lone, I walk a...

𝄋 Chorus

C5 G5* D5 E5 C5 G5*

My shad - ow's the on - ly one that walks be - side me. My shal - low heart's

© 2004 WB MUSIC CORP. and GREEN DAZE MUSIC
All Rights Administered by WB MUSIC CORP.
All Rights Reserved Used by Permission

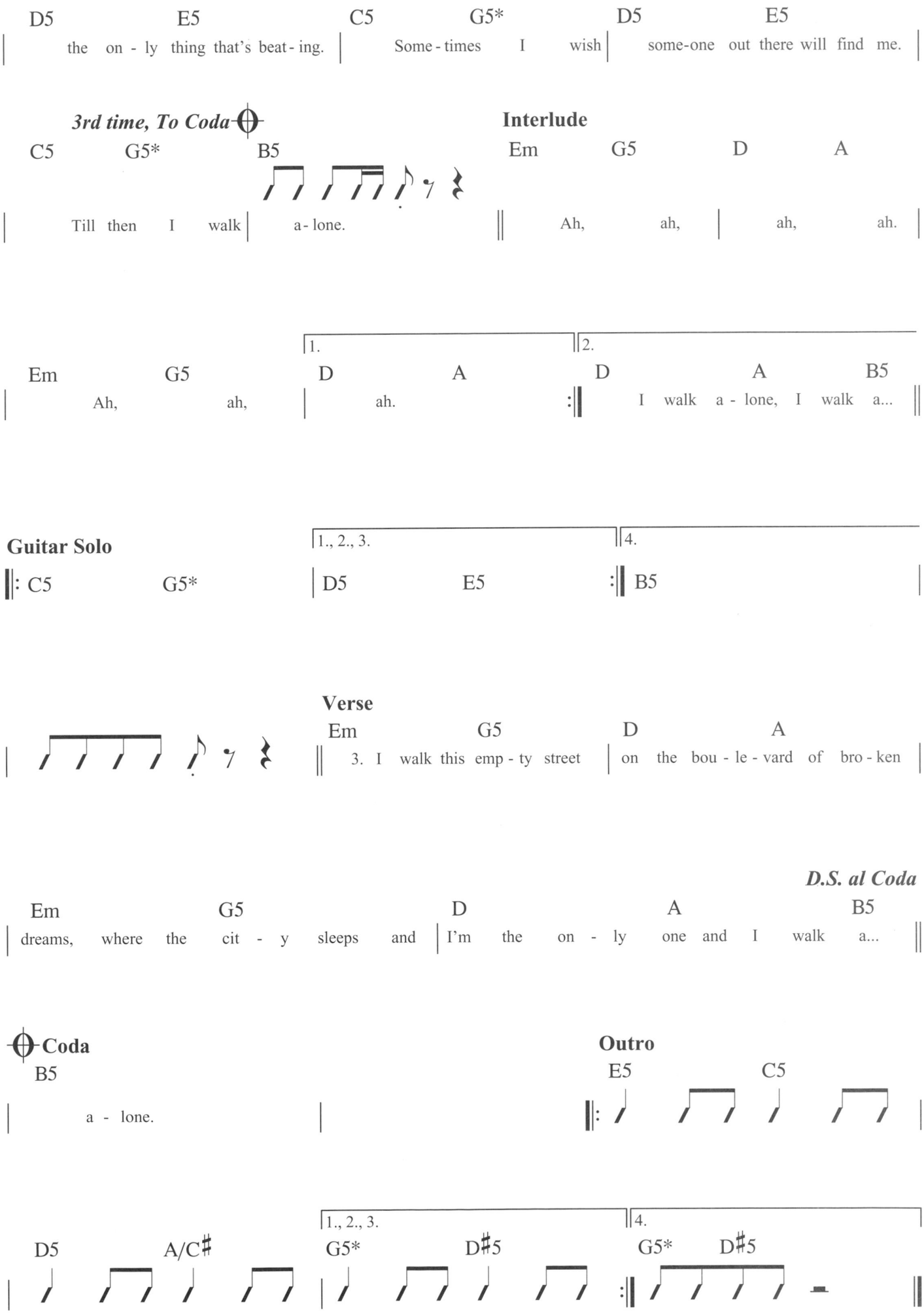
D5 E5 C5 G5* D5 E5
the on - ly thing that's beat - ing. Some - times I wish some-one out there will find me.
3rd time, To Coda
C5 G5* B5
Till then I walk a - lone.
Interlude
Em G5 D A
Ah, ah, ah, ah.
1. 2.
Em G5 D A D A B5
Ah, ah, ah. I walk a - lone, I walk a...
Guitar Solo
1., 2., 3. 4.
C5 G5* D5 E5 B5
Verse
Em G5 D A
3. I walk this emp - ty street on the bou - le - vard of bro - ken
D.S. al Coda
Em G5 D A B5
dreams, where the cit - y sleeps and I'm the on - ly one and I walk a...
Coda
B5
a - lone.
Outro
E5 C5
1., 2., 3. 4.
D5 A/C♯ G5* D♯5 G5* D♯5

Breaking the Girl

Words and Music by Anthony Kiedis, Flea, John Frusciante and Chad Smith

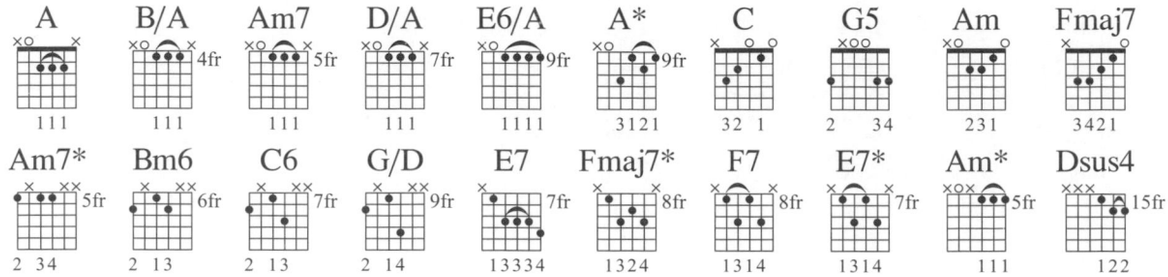

Tune down 1/2 step:
(low to high) E♭-A♭-D♭-G♭-B♭-E♭

Key of A

Intro

Slow, in 2 (♩♩ = ♩♩)

A | B/A Am7 | D/A

Verse

E6/A A* | A | B/A Am7

1. I am a man
2. Raised by my dad,

D/A | E6/A A* | A

cut from the know. Rare - ly do
girl of the day. He was my

B/A Am7 | D/A | E6/A A*

friends come and then go.
man, that was the way.

A | B/A Am7 | D/A

She was the girl soft but es -
She was the girl left a -

E6/A A* | A | B/A Am7

tranged. We were the two, our
lone. Feel - ing no need to

D/A | E6/A A*

lives re - ar - ranged.
make me her home.

© 1991 MOEBETOBLAME MUSIC
All Rights Reserved Used by Permission

Pre-Chorus

C G5 Am

Feel - ing so good that day.
I don't know what, when or why

C G5 Fmaj7

A feel - ing of love that day.
the twi - light of love had ar - rived.

𝄋 Chorus

Am7* Bm6 C6 G/D E7

Twist - ing and turn - ing, your feel - ings are burn - ing, you're break - ing the girl.

Am7* Bm6 C6 G/D Fmaj7*

She meant you no harm.

Am7* Bm6 C6 G/D E7

Think you're so clev - er, but now you must sev - er, you're break - ing the girl.

3rd time, To Coda ⊕

Am7* Bm6 C6 G/D Fmaj7* F7 E7*

He loves no one else.

Interlude ***8th time, D.S. al Coda***

Am* *Dsus4 *Play 8 times*

*Bass plays C.

⊕ Coda

Outro

Am7* Bm6 C6 G/D E7

Repeat and fade

Am7* Bm6 C6 G/D Fmaj7*

Bye Bye Love

Words and Music by Felice Bryant and Boudleaux Bryant

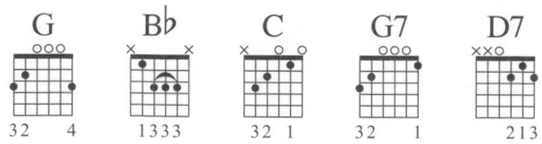

Capo II

Key of A (Capo Key of G)

Intro

Moderately fast (♩♩ = ♩♪)

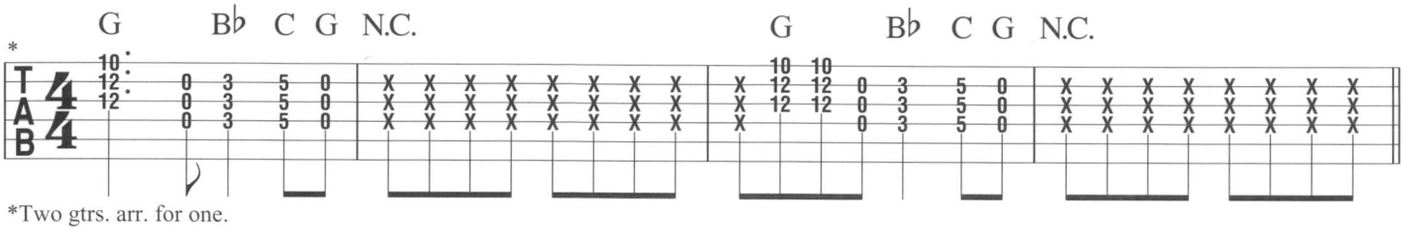

*Two gtrs. arr. for one.

Chorus

C G C G G7

|: Bye, bye, love. | Bye, bye, hap | - pi - ness. |

C G D7 G G7

| Hel - lo lone | - li - ness. I | think a I'm a gon - na cry. | |

C G C G G7

| Bye, bye, love. | Bye, bye, sweet | ca - ress. |

C G D7 G

| Hel - lo emp | - ti - ness. I | feel like I could die. | A bye, bye, |

Copyright © 1957 by HOUSE OF BRYANT PUBLICATIONS, Gatlinburg, TN
Copyright Renewed
All Foreign Rights Controlled by SONY/ATV MUSIC PUBLISHING LLC
All Rights for SONY/ATV MUSIC PUBLISHING LLC Administered by
SONY/ATV MUSIC PUBLISHING LLC, 424 Church Street, Suite 1200, Nashville, TN 37219
International Copyright Secured All Rights Reserved

3rd time, To Coda ⊕

D7 G

my love, good - bye. | 1. There goes my
2. I'm a through with ||

Verse

D7 G

ba - by with a some - one new. | She sure looks hap -
ro - mance. I'm a through with love. | I'm through with a

D7 G G7

- py. I sure am blue. | She was my
count - in' the stars a - bove. | And here's the

C D7

ba - by till he stepped in. | Good - bye to
rea - son that I'm so free: | my lov - in'

2nd time, D.S. al Coda 2

G G7

ro - mance, nn, that might have been. | :||
ba - by is a through with me. |

⊕ **Coda** **Outro** *Repeat and fade*

G G D7 G

A bye, bye, ||: my love, good - bye. | A, bye, bye, :||

Champagne Supernova

Words and Music by Noel Gallagher

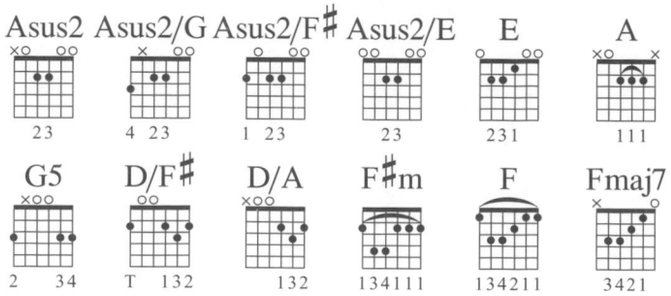

Key of A

Intro

Moderately slow

Asus2 | Asus2/G | Asus2/F♯ | Asus2/E

etc.

Verse

Asus2 | Asus2/G

1., 3., 4. How man - y spe - cial peo - ple change? | How man - y lives are liv - ing strange?
2. Wake up the dawn and ask her why a | dream - er dreams she nev - er dies.

4th time, To Coda 2

Asus2/F♯ | Asus2/E | Asus2

Where were you while we were get - ing high? / Wipe that tear a - way now from your eye. | Slow-ly walk-ing down the hall,

Asus2/G | Asus2/F♯

fast - er than a can - non ball. | Where were you while we were get - ting high?

Chorus

*(E) Asus2/E | (A) Asus2 | (G5) Asus2/G

Some day you will | find me caught be - neath the land | - slide in a cham-

*2nd & 3rd times, substitute chords in parentheses.

(D/F♯) Asus2/F♯ | (E) Asus2/E | (A) Asus2

- pagne su - per-no - va in the sky. | Some - day you will | find me caught be - neath the land-

(G5) Asus2/G | (D/F♯) Asus2/F♯ | 1. Asus2/E

- slide in a cham | - pagne su - per no - va, a | cham - pagne su - per - no - va in the sky.

Copyright © 1995 Sony/ATV Music Publishing UK Limited and Oasis Music
All Rights Administered by Sony/ATV Music Publishing LLC, 424 Church Street, Suite 1200, Nashville, TN 37219
International Copyright Secured All Rights Reserved

Interlude

| Asus2 | Asus2/G | Asus2/F♯ | Asus2/E :‖

2., 3.

Bridge

E G5

| cham-pagne su - per-no - va. 'Cos ‖ peo - ple be - lieve that they're | gon - na get a - way for the sum- |

A G5

| - mer. | But | you and I, we live and die. The |

2nd time, To Coda 1 ⊕ *D.C. al Coda 1 (take repeat)*

D/A E

| world's still spin-ning 'round, we don't know why, | | why, why, why, why. ‖

⊕ **Coda 1** **Guitar Solo**

A G5

| why, why, why, why. ‖: | |

D.C. al Coda 2 (take repeat)

Play 4 times

| F♯m | F G5 :‖ F G5 | F G5 ‖

⊕ **Coda 2**

Asus2/E Asus2 Asus2/G

| We were get-ting high. ‖: We were get-ting high. | We were get-ting high. |

Outro

Asus2/F♯ Asus2/E Asus2 Asus2/G

| We were get-ting high. | We were get-ting high. :‖ | |

Asus2/F♯ Fmaj7 G5 A

grad. slower

| | | | ‖

Crazy Little Thing Called Love

Words and Music by Freddie Mercury

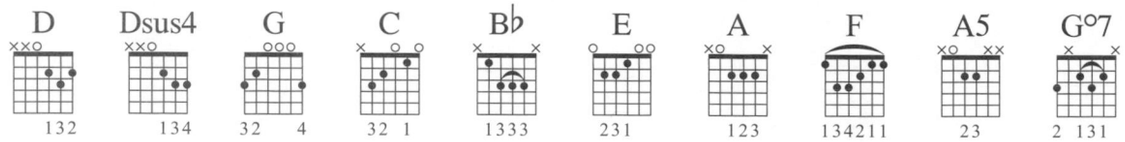

Key of D

Intro

Moderately fast (♩♩ = ♩ ♪)

D Dsus4 D *Play 3 times* Dsus4 D

etc.

1. This thing

Verse

D Dsus4 D Dsus4 D G

(5.) called love, called love, | I just it cries | can't in a

3. *See additional lyrics*

C G D Dsus4 D Dsus4 D

han - dle it. This thing cra - dle all night. It swings, | called love, it jives, | I must

G C G D

shakes all o - ver like a get 'round | jel - ly to - fish. it. | I ain't read I kind - a like | - y. it.

3rd time, To Coda 1

4th time, To Coda 2

1. 2.

B♭ C D

Cra-zy lit - tle thing called love. | 2. A, this thing | There goes my

Bridge

G C G

ba - by, | she knows how to rock and roll. | She drives me

B♭ E A F N.C.

cra - zy. | She gives me hot and cold fe - ver, she leaves me in a cool, cool sweat.

D.S. al Coda 1

E A N.C.

3. I've got - ta be cool

© 1979 QUEEN MUSIC LTD.
All Rights for the U.S. and Canada Controlled and Administered by BEECHWOOD MUSIC CORP.
All Rights for the world excluding the U.S. and Canada Controlled and Administered by EMI MUSIC PUBLISHING LTD.
All Rights Reserved International Copyright Secured Used by Permission

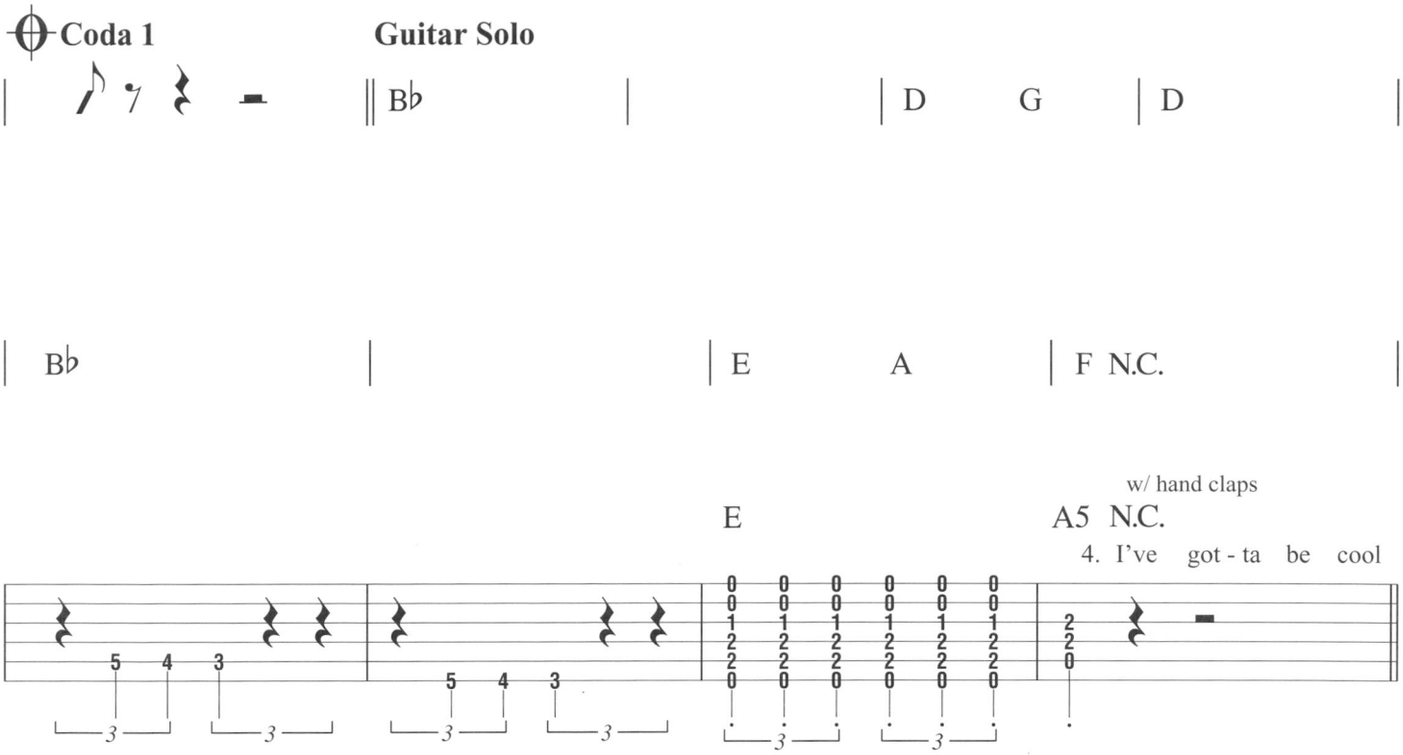

Verse

N.C. *(E)

ah, re - lax, get hip, and get on my tracks. Take a

*Implied by background vocals.

(F) (E) (F) (G) (C) (G°7) (G)

back - seat, hitch - hike, and take a long ride on my mo - tor - bike un - til I'm

(F) (E) (F)

read - y. Cra - zy lit - tle thing called love. (Drums enter) (Bass enters) 5. This thing

D.S. al Coda 2

Coda 2 ***Repeat and fade***

B♭ C D

Cra - zy lit - tle thing called love.

Additional Lyrics

3. I've gotta be cool, relax,
Get hip, get on my tracks
Take a backseat, hitch-hike,
Take a long ride on my motorbike
Until I'm ready.
Crazy little thing called love.

Daughters

Words and Music by John Mayer

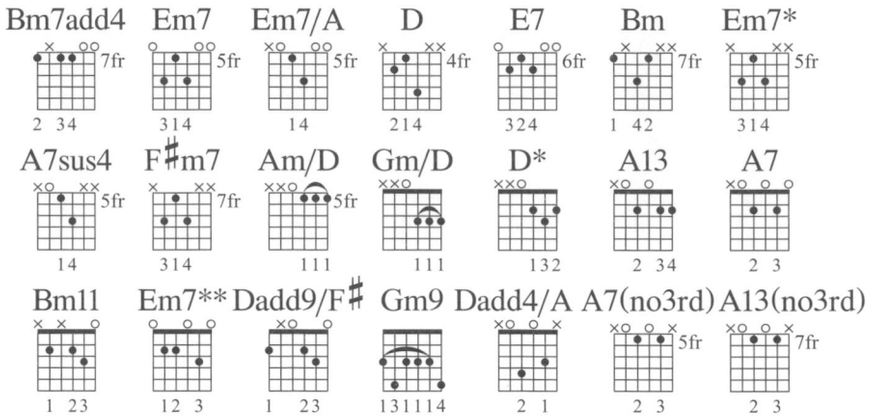

Key of D

Intro

Slow, in 2 (♩♩ = ♪♪)

Bm7add4 Em7 Em7/A D

6/8 | etc. | :

Verse

Bm7add4 Em7 Em7/A D

1. I know a girl; she puts the col - or in - side of my world. But

Bm7add4 Em7 Em7/A D

she's just like a maze where all of the walls all con - tin - ual - ly change. And

Bm7add4 Em7 Em7/A D

I've done all I can to stand on her steps with my heart in my hand. Now

Bm7add4 Em7 Em7/A D

I'm start - ing to see may - be it's got noth - ing to do with me.

𝄋 Chorus

Bm7add4 E7 Em7/A D Bm7add4 E7 Em7/A D

Fa - thers, be good to your daugh - ters. Daugh-ters will love like you do.

3rd time, To Coda 2 ***To Coda 1***

Bm7add4 E7 Em7/A D Bm7add4 E7 Em7/A D

Girls be - come lov - ers who turn in - to moth - ers. So moth - ers, be good to your daugh - ters, too.

Copyright © 2003 Sony/ATV Music Publishing LLC and Specific Harm Music
All Rights Administered by Sony/ATV Music Publishing LLC, 424 Church Street, Suite 1200, Nashville, TN 37219
International Copyright Secured All Rights Reserved

Interlude

Bm | Em7* | A7sus4 | D | Em7* F♯m7

etc.

Verse

Bm | Em7* | A7sus4 | D | Em7* F♯m7

2. Oh, you see that | skin? It's the | same she's been stand - in' | in since the |

D.S. al Coda 1

Bm | Em7* | A7sus4 | D | Em7* F♯m7

day she saw him | walk-ing a - way. Now she's | left clean-ing up the mess he | made. So ||

Coda 1

Bridge

Am/D | Gm/D | D* | A13 | A7 | Bm11

Boys, you can | break. You'll | find out how much they can | take. Boys will be |

Em7** | Dadd9/F♯ | Gm9 | A7 | Dadd4/A

strong, and boys sol - dier | on, but boys would be | gone with - out warmth from a | wom - an's |

Interlude

A7(no3rd) A13(no3rd) | Bm7add4 | E7 | Em7/A | D | Em7/A | D

good, good heart. ||: | :|| On be - half of |

D.S. al Coda 2

Bm7add4 | E7 | Em7/A | D | Bm7add4 | E7 | Em7/A | D

ev-'ry man look-ing out for | ev-'ry girl, you are the | god and the weight of her | world. So ||

Coda 2

Em7/A | D | Bm7add4 | E7 | Em7/A | D | Em7/A | D

2nd time, grad. slower

daugh - ters, too. So ||: moth - ers, be good to your | daugh - ters, too. So :|| daugh - ters, too. ||

Every Rose Has Its Thorn

Words and Music by Bobby Dall, C.C. Deville, Bret Michaels and Rikki Rockett

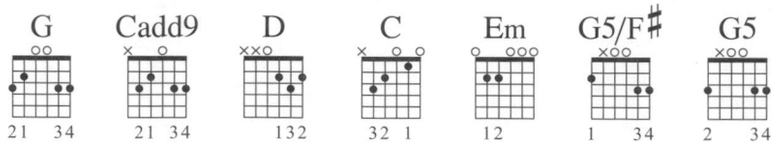

Tune down 1/2 step:
(low to high) E♭-A♭-D♭-G♭-B♭-E♭

Key of G

Intro

Slow

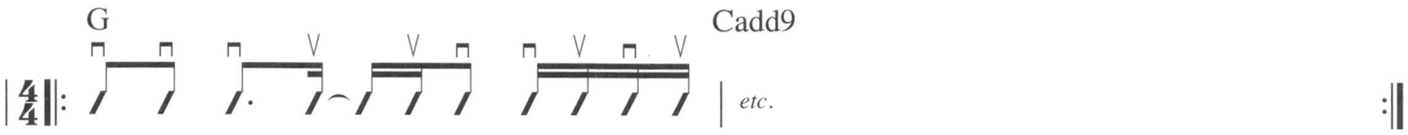

Verse

G Cadd9

1. We both lie si - lent and still in the | dead of the night. Al - though we
lis - ten to our fav - 'rite song play - in' on the | ra - di - o. Hear the d.
3. I know I could-a saved a love that night if I'd known what to say.

G Cadd9

both lie close to - geth - er, we feel | miles a - part in - side. Was it some-
j. say love's a game of eas - y come and | eas - y go. But I won-
'Stead of mak - in' love, we both made our sep - 'rate ways. And now I

G Cadd9 G Cadd9

- thin' I said or some - thin' I did? Did my words | not come out right? Though I tried
- der, does he know? Has he ev | - er felt like this? And I know
hear you found some - bod - y new and that I nev - er meant that much to you. To

D C

not to hurt you, though I tried. | But I guess that's why they say
that you'd be here right now if I | could-a let you know some - how. I guess
hear that tears me up in - side and to see you cuts me like a knife. I guess

Chorus

G Cadd9 G

ev - 'ry rose has its thorn, | just like ev | - 'ry night has its dawn.

Cadd9 G D Cadd9 G

Just like ev | - 'ry cow - boy sings a sad, | sad song,

3rd time, To Coda

1.

Cadd9

ev - 'ry rose has its thorn. | *Spoken: Yeah, it does.*

Copyright © 1988 by Cyanide Publishing
All Rights in the United States Administered by Universal Music - Z Songs
International Copyright Secured All Rights Reserved

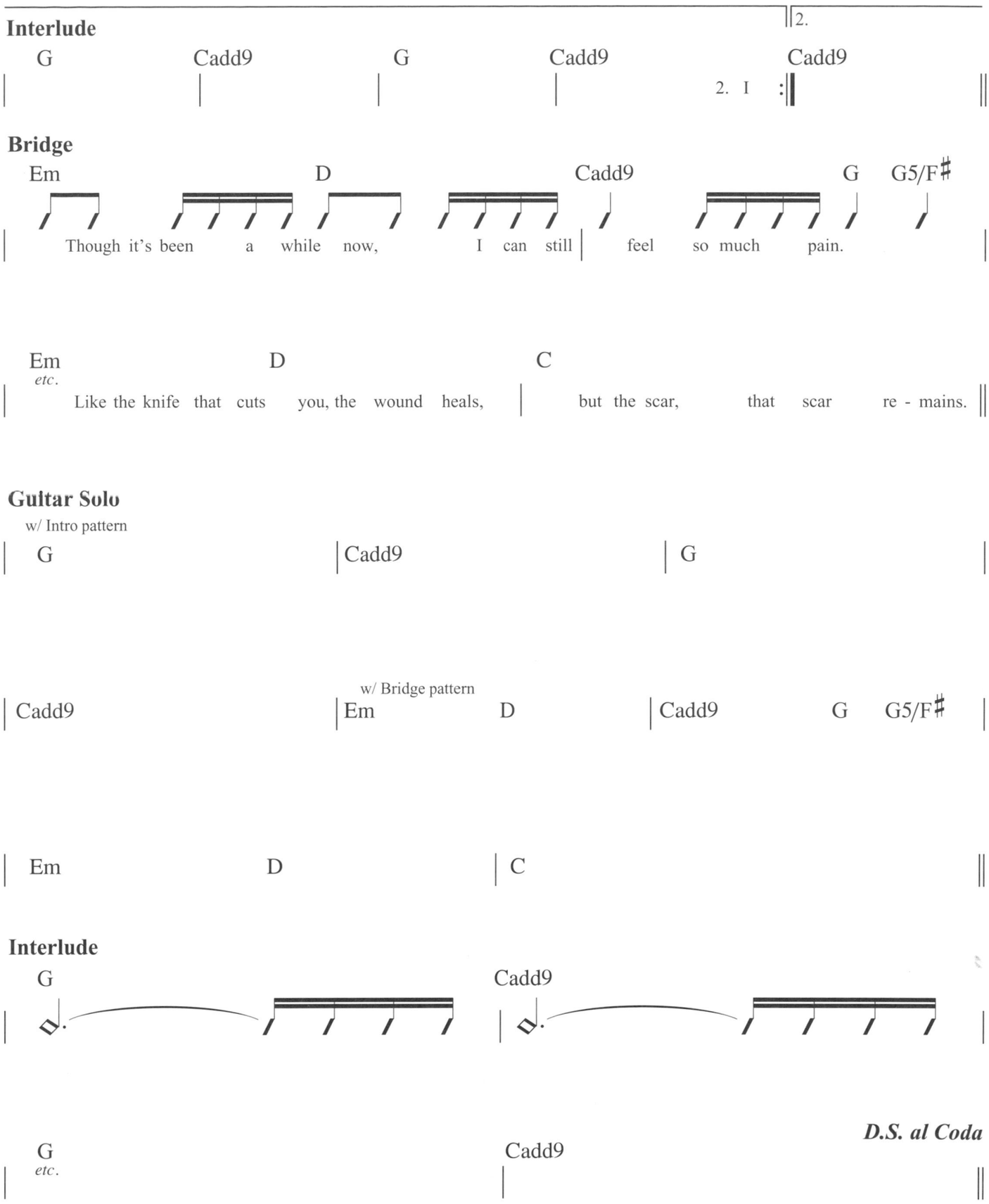
Interlude
2.
G Cadd9 G Cadd9 Cadd9
2. I
Bridge
Em D Cadd9 G G5/F♯
Though it's been a while now, I can still feel so much pain.
Em D C
etc.
Like the knife that cuts you, the wound heals, but the scar, that scar re - mains.
Guitar Solo
w/ Intro pattern
G Cadd9 G
w/ Bridge pattern
Cadd9 Em D Cadd9 G G5/F♯
Em D C
Interlude
G Cadd9
D.S. al Coda
G Cadd9
etc.
Coda
Cadd9 N.C.(D) G5
grad. slower

Falling Slowly

from the Motion Picture ONCE
from the Broadway Musical ONCE

Words and Music by Glen Hansard and Marketa Irglova

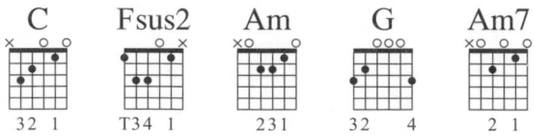

Key of C

Intro

Slow

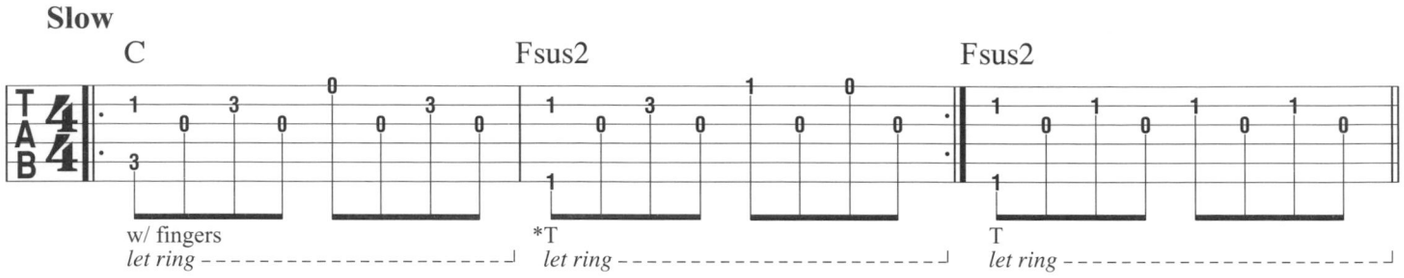

*T = Thumb on 6th string

Verse

C — Fsus2

Male: 1. I don't know you, but I want you
Both: 2. Fall - ing slow - ly, eyes that know me

C — Fsus2 — C

all the more for that. — ** *Male & Female:* Words fall through me and
and I can't go back. — And moods that take me

**Hereafter referred to as *Both*.

Fsus2 — C — Fsus2

al - ways fool me, — and I can't re - act. — *Male:* And
and e - rase me — and I'm paint - ed black. — *Male:* Well,

Pre-Chorus

Am — G — Fsus2 — G — Am — G

games that nev - er a - mount to more than they're meant will play them - selves
you have suf - fered e - nough and warred with your - self. It's time that you

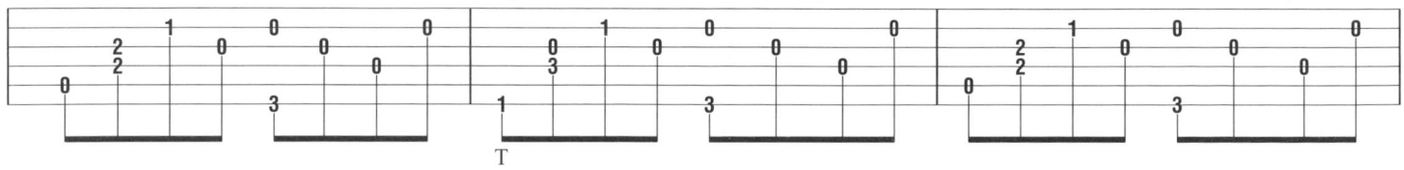

Fsus2

out.
won.

© 2006 THE SWELL SEASON PUBLISHING
All Rights Administered by WB MUSIC CORP.
Exclusive Worldwide Print Rights Administered by ALFRED MUSIC
All Rights Reserved Used by Permission

Chorus

C — *etc.* — Fsus2 — Am7

Both: Take this sink - in' | boat and point it | home, we've still got

Fsus2 — C — Fsus2

time. | Raise your hope - ful | voice, you have a

1. | 2.

Am7 — Fsus2 — C

choice. { You'll make / You've made } it | now. | :‖ Fall - ing slow - ly,

Fsus2 — Am7 — Fsus2

sing your mel - o - | dy. I'll sing it | loud. ‖

Outro

w/ Voc. ad lib.

C | Fsus2 | Am7

Fsus2

To come, | I paid the

cost too late, | now you're | gone.

C — Fsus2 — C

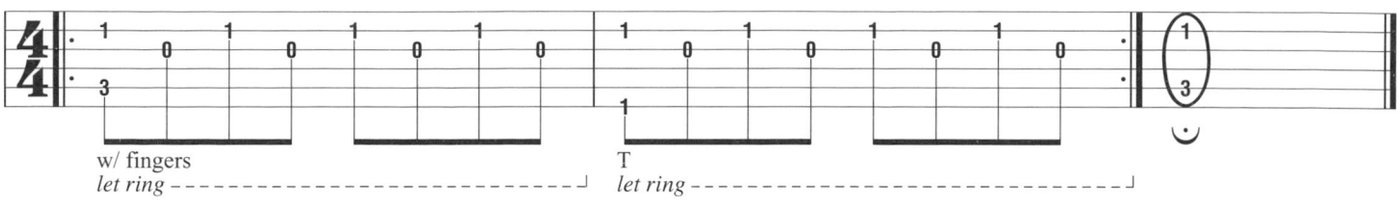

Fast Car

Words and Music by Tracy Chapman

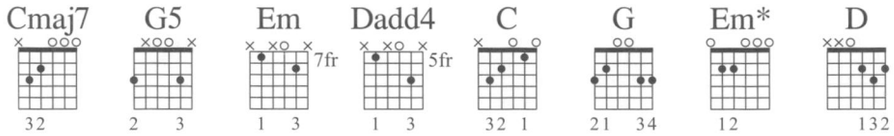

Capo II

Key of A (Capo Key of G)

Intro

Moderately

1., 2. | 3. | 4.

Cmaj7 G5 Em Dadd4 Em Dadd4 Em Dadd4

Riff **End Riff**

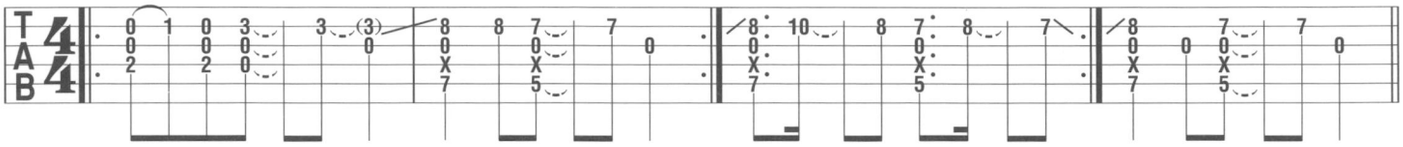

Verse

w/ Intro riff

Cmaj7 G5 Em Dadd4

1. You got a fast car, I want a tick - et to an - y - where.
2. You got a fast car. I got a plan to get us out of here. I been

3. - 7. *See additional lyrics*

4th time, skip to Interlude 1

7th time, To Coda

Cmaj7 G5 Em Dadd4

May - be we make a deal, may - be to - geth - er we can get some - where.
work-ing at the con - ven - ience store, man-aged to save just a lit - tle bit of mon - ey.

Cmaj7 G5 Em Dadd4

An - y - place is bet - ter. Start - ing from ze - ro, got noth - ing to lose.
Won't have to drive too far, just 'cross the bor - der and in - to the cit - y.

Cmaj7 G5 Em Dadd4

May - be we'll make some - thing; Me, my - self, I got noth - ing to prove.
You and I can both get jobs and fi - nal - ly see what it means to be liv - ing.

Interlude 1

1., 2., 3. | 4., 5., 6.

Cmaj7 G5 Em Dadd4 Cmaj7 G5 Em Dadd4 Em Dadd4

'Cause I re-mem-ber when we were

© 1987 EMI APRIL MUSIC INC. and PURPLE RABBIT MUSIC
All Rights Reserved International Copyright Secured Used by Permission

Chorus

C G

driv - in', driv-ing in your car, the | speed so fast I felt like I was drunk.

Em* D

Cit - y lights lay out be - fore us, and your | arm felt nice wrapped 'round my shoul-der. And

C Em* D C Em*

I, I had a | feel - ing that I be-longed. | I, I had a

Interlude 2

w/ Intro riff

D C D Cmaj7 G5

feel - ing I could be some - one, | be some - one, be some - one. ||

1st & 2nd time, D.S.
3rd time, D.S. al Coda

Em Dadd4 | Cmaj7 G5 | Em Dadd4 ||

Coda

Outro

Cmaj7 G5 Em Dadd4 Cmaj7 G5

Play 3 times

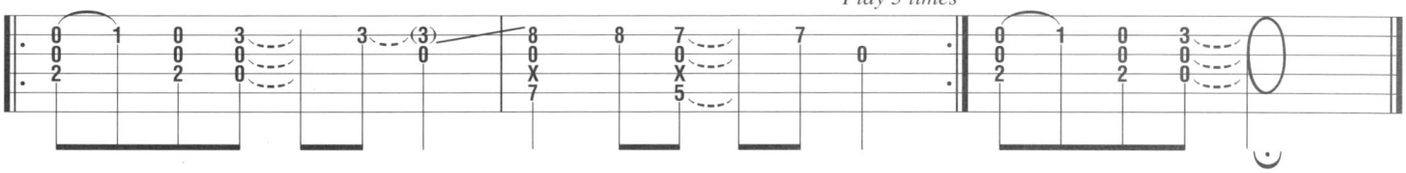

Additional Lyrics

3. You see, my old man's got a problem.
   He live with the bottle, that's the way it is.
   He says his body's too old for working;
   His body's too young to look like his.
   My mama went off and left him;
   She wanted more from life than he could give.
   I said somebody's got to take care of him.
   So I quit school and that's what I did.

4. You got a fast car,
   But is it fast enough so we can fly away?
   We gotta make a decision:
   Leave tonight or live and die this way.
   (To Interlude 1)

5. You got a fast car.
   We go cruising to entertain ourselves.
   You still ain't got a job
   And I work in the market as a checkout girl.
   I know things will get better;
   You'll find work and I'll get promoted.
   We'll move out of the shelter,
   Buy a big house and live in the suburbs.

6. You got a fast car.
   I got a job that pays all our bills.
   You stay out drinking late at the bar,
   See more of your friends than you do of your kids.
   I'd always hoped for better,
   Thought maybe together you and me'd find it.
   I got no plans, I ain't going nowhere,
   So take your fast car and keep on driving.

7. You got a fast car.
   Is it fast enough so you can fly away?
   You gotta make a decision:
   Leave tonight or live and die this way.

Free Fallin'

Words and Music by Tom Petty and Jeff Lynne

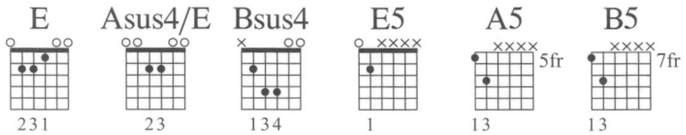

Key of E

Intro

Moderately slow

E Asus2/E E Bsus4 E Asus2/E E Bsus4

etc. 1. She's a

Verse

E Asus2/E E Bsus4

good girl, loves her ma - ma, loves

E Asus2/E E Bsus4 E Asus2/E E Bsus4

etc.

Je - sus, and A - mer - i - ca, too. She's a good girl, cra - zy 'bout El - vis, loves

E Asus2/E E Bsus4 E Asus2/E E Bsus4

hors - es and her boy - friend, too. 2. And it's a

Verse

E Asus2/E E Bsus4

long day liv - in' in Re - se - da. There's a
vam - pires walk - in' through the val - ley move
glide down o - ver Mul - hol - land, I wan - na

E Asus2/E E Bsus4

free - way run - nin' through the yard. And I'm a
west down Ven - tu - ra Bou - le - vard. And all the
write her name in the sky. I'm gon - na

E Asus2/E E Bsus4

bad boy 'cause I don't e - ven miss her. I'm a
bad boys are stand - in' in the shad - ows. And the
free fall out in - to noth - in', gon - na

3rd time, To Coda

E Asus2/E E Bsus4

bad boy for break - in' her heart. And
good girls are home with bro - ken hearts. Now I'm
leave this world for a while. Now

Copyright © 1989 Gone Gator Music and EMI April Music Inc.
All Rights Reserved Used by Permission

Chorus

E Asus2/E | free, | E Bsus4 | free | E Asus2/E | fall - in'. | E Bsus4 | Yeah, I'm |

E Asus2/E | free, | E Bsus4 | free | E Asus2/E | fall - in'. | E Bsus4 | 3. Now all the :‖ 1. | E Bsus4 | ‖ 2.

Interlude

E Asus2/E | E Bsus4 | E Asus2/E | (Free fall - in', I'm a | E Bsus4 | free fall - in', I'm a... |

D.S. al Coda

E Asus2/E | E Bsus4 | E Asus2/E | Free fall - in', I'm a | E Bsus4 | free fall - in', I'm...) 4. I wan-na ‖

Coda

Chorus

E Asus2/E | free, (Fall - in', I'm a | E Bsus4 | free free fall - in', I'm a | E Asus2/E | fall - in'. free fall - in', I'm a |

E Bsus4 | Yeah, I'm free fall - in', I'm a... | E Asus2/E | free, Fall - in', I'm a | E Bsus4 | free free fall - in', I'm a |

Interlude

E Asus2/E | fall - in'. free fall - in', I'm a | E Bsus4 | free fall - in', I'm a...) ‖ E5 A5 | / / /– / / / / / |

E5 B5 | /–/ /–/ / / / /— | E5 A5 | /–/ /–/ / / / / | E5 B5 | /–/ /–/ / / / /— |

| | (Free fall - in', I'm a | free Yeah, I'm fall - in', I'm a...) ‖

Outro-Chorus ***Repeat and fade***

‖: E Asus2/E | free, * (Free fall - in', I'm a | E Bsus4 | free free fall - in', I'm a, | E Asus2/E | fall - in'. free fall - in', I'm a | E Bsus4 | Oh! free fall - in', I'm a...) :‖

*Bkgds enter 2nd time.

Have You Ever Seen the Rain?

Words and Music by John Fogerty

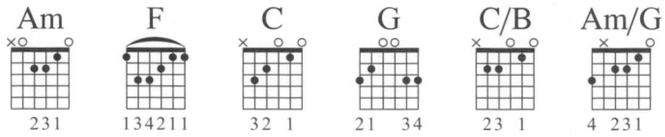

Key of C

Intro

Moderately

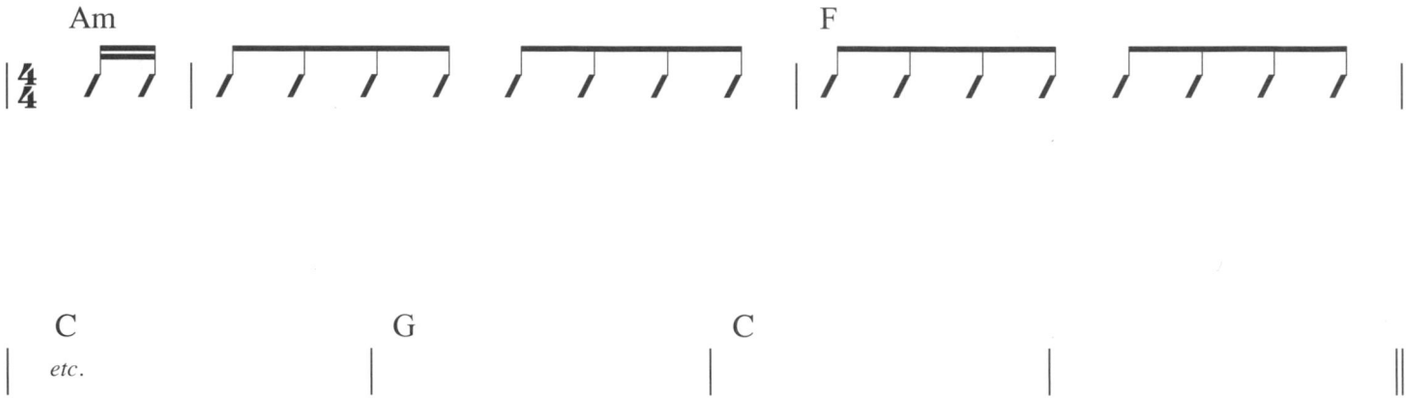

Verse

C

1. Some-one told me long a-go, there's a calm be-fore the storm. I know, it's been com-in' for some time. When it's o-ver, so they say, it'-ll rain a sun-ny day. I know;
2. Yes-ter-day and days be-fore, sun is cold and rain is hard. I know, been that way for all my time. Till for-ev-er, on it goes, through the cir-cle, fast and slow. I know;

G

Copyright © 1970 Jondora Music
Copyright Renewed
International Copyright Secured All Rights Reserved

G C

shin - in' down like wa - ter.
it can't stop, I won - der.

Chorus

F G C *(C/B) Am **(Am/G)

I want to know, have you ev - er seen the rain?

*Optional: Bass plays B. **Optional: Bass plays G.

F G C (C/B) Am (Am/G)

I want to know, have you ev - er seen the rain

1. 2.

F G C

com - in' down a sun - ny day?

F G C (C/B) Am (Am/G)

I want to know, have you ev - er seen the rain?

F G C (C/B) Am (Am/G)

I want to know, have you ev - er seen the rain

F G C G C

com - in' down a sun - ny day?

Hey There Delilah

Words and Music by Tom Higgenson

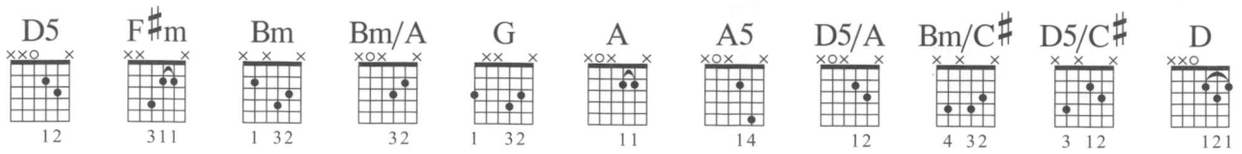

Key of D

Intro

Moderately

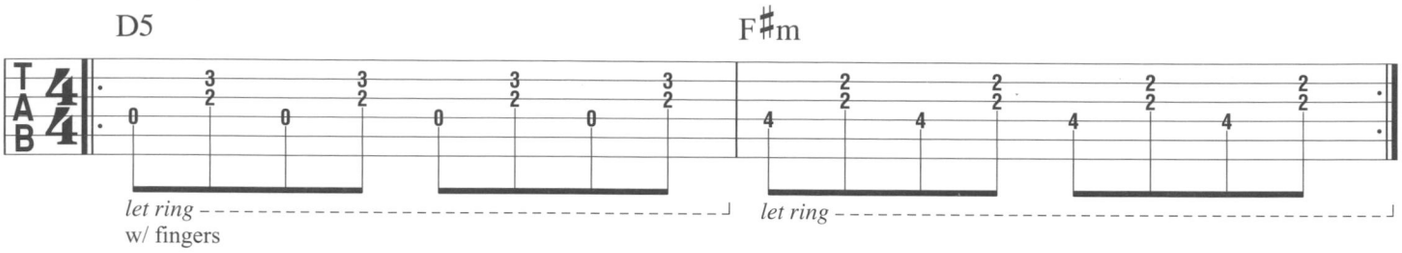

Verse

D5 F♯m D5

etc.

1. Hey there, De - li - lah, what's it | like in New York Cit - y? I'm a | thou-sand miles a - way, but girl, to -
2. Hey there, De - li - lah, I know | times are get - tin' hard, but just be - | lieve me, girl, some-day I'll pay the

F♯m Bm Bm/A G A

night you look so pret - ty. Yes you | do. | Times Square can't shine as bright as
bills with this gui - tar. We'll have it | good. | We'll have the life we knew we

Bm A A5 D5

you, I swear it's | true. | Hey there, De - li - lah, don't you
would, my word is | good. | Hey there, De - li - lah, I've got

F♯m D5 F♯m

wor-ry a - bout the dis-tance. I'm right | there; if you get lone - ly, give this | song an - oth - er lis - ten. Close your
so much left to say. If ev - 'ry | sim - ple song I wrote to you would | take your breath a - way, I'd write it

Bm Bm/A G A Bm

eyes, | lis - ten to my voice, it's my dis - | guise. I'm by your
all. | E - ven more in love with me you'd | fall, we'd have it

𝄋 Chorus

A A5 D5 D5/A Bm Bm/C♯ D5 D5/A

side. || Oh, it's what you do to | me. | Oh, it's what you do to
all. ||

3rd time, To Coda

Bm Bm/C♯ D5 D5/A Bm Bm/C♯ D5 D5/A

me. | Oh, it's what you do to | me. | Oh, it's what you do to

1. Bm Bm/C♯ D5 D5/A

me, what you do to | me. :||

2. Bm Bm/A

me. A ||

© 2005 WB MUSIC CORP., FEARMORE MUSIC and SO HAPPY PUBLISHING
All Rights Administered by WB MUSIC CORP.
All Rights Reserved Used by Permission

Bridge

G A D5 D5/A
thou-sand miles seems pret-ty far, but they've got planes and trains and cars. I'd walk to you if I had no oth-er

Bm Bm/A G A
way. Our friends would all make fun of us and we'll just laugh a-long be-cause we

D5 D5/C♯ Bm Bm/A G
know that none of them have felt this way. De- li-lah, I can prom-ise you that

A Bm
by the time that we get through, the world will nev-er ev-er be the same, and you're to

Verse

A A5 D5
blame. 3. Hey there, De-li-lah, you be

F♯m D5 F♯m
good and don't you miss me. Two more years and you'll be done with school and I'll be mak-in' his-t'ry like I

Bm Bm/A G A Bm Bm/A
do. You'll know it's all be-cause of you.

G A Bm Bm/A G A
We can do what-ev-er we want to. Hey there, De-li-lah, here's to

D.S. al Coda

Bm A A5
you, this one's for you.

Coda **Outro** 1. - 4. 5.

w/ Voc. ad lib.

Bm Bm/C♯ D5 D5/A Bm Bm/C♯ D
me, what you do to me.

Ho Hey

Words and Music by Jeremy Fraites and Wesley Schultz

Key of C

Intro

Moderately slow

C F/C C F/C C F/C C F/C

etc.

(*Ho!* | *Hey!* | *Ho!* | *Hey!*)

Verse

C F/C C F/C

1. (*Ho!*) I've been try'n' to do it right; (*Hey!*) I've been liv - in' a lone - ly life.
2. (*Ho!*) So show me fam - i - ly, (*Hey!*) all the blood that I will bleed.

C F/C C

(*Ho!*) I've been sleep - in' here in - stead; (*Hey!*) I've been sleep - in' in my bed,
(*Ho!*) I don't know where I be - long, (*Hey!*) I don't know where I went wrong,

Am G F/C C F/C C F/C

(*Ho!*) I've been sleep - in' in my bed. (*Hey!* | *Ho!*)
(*Ho!*) but I can write a song.

1. 2.

C

(*Hey! Two, three.*) I be - long with

Chorus

Double-time feel

Am G

you, you be - long with me; you're my sweet -

End double-time feel

C Am G F/C

- heart. I be - long with you, you be - long with me; you're my sweet...

Copyright © 2011 The Lumineers
All Rights Exclusively Administered by Songs Of Kobalt Music Publishing
All Rights Reserved Used by Permission

Interlude

w/ Intro pattern

To Coda

C F/C C F/C C F/C C F/C

(Ho! *Hey!* *Ho!* *Hey!)*

Verse

C F/C C F/C

3. *(Ho!)* I don't think you're right for him. *(Hey!)* Look at what it might have been if you

C F/C C Am G F/C

(Ho!) took a bus to Chi - na town. *(Hey!)* I'd be stand-in' on Ca-nal *(Ho!)* and Bow - er-y.

C Am G F/C C

(Hey! *Ho!)* And she'd be stand-in' next to me. *(Hey! Two, three.)* I be-long with

Chorus

Double-time feel

w/ Chorus pattern

1. 2.

Am G C C

you, you be-long with me; you're my sweet - heart. I be-long with - heart.

Bridge

F/C C Gsus4 C F/C C Gsus4

Love, we need it now. Let's hope for some. 'Cause

D.S. al Coda **Coda**

F/C C Gsus4 C C

oh, we're bleed - in' out. I be-long with *Hey!)*

A Horse with No Name

Words and Music by Dewey Bunnell

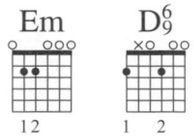

Key of Em

Intro

Moderately (♩♩ = ♩♪)

Em D6/9 Em D6/9

etc. 1. On the

*Two gtrs. arr. for one.

Verse

Em D6/9 Em

etc.

first part of the jour - ney I was look - ing at all the life.
two days in the des - ert sun my skin be - gan to turn

3. *See additional lyrics*

D6/9 Em D6/9

There were plants and birds and rocks and things. There was
red. Af - ter three days in the des - ert fun I was

Em D6/9 Em

sand and hills and rains. The first thing I met was a
look - ing at a riv - er bed. And the sto - ry it told of a

2nd time, skip to Chorus

D6/9 Em D6/9

fly with a buzz and the sky with no clouds. The
riv - er that flowed made me sad to think it was dead. You see, I've

Em D6/9 Em

heat was hot and the ground was dry, but the air was full of sounds.

Chorus

D6/9 Em D6/9

I've been through the des - ert on a horse with no name. It felt

© 1972 (Renewed) WARNER/CHAPPELL MUSIC LTD.
All Rights for the Western Hemisphere Controlled by WB MUSIC CORP.
All Rights Reserved Used by Permission

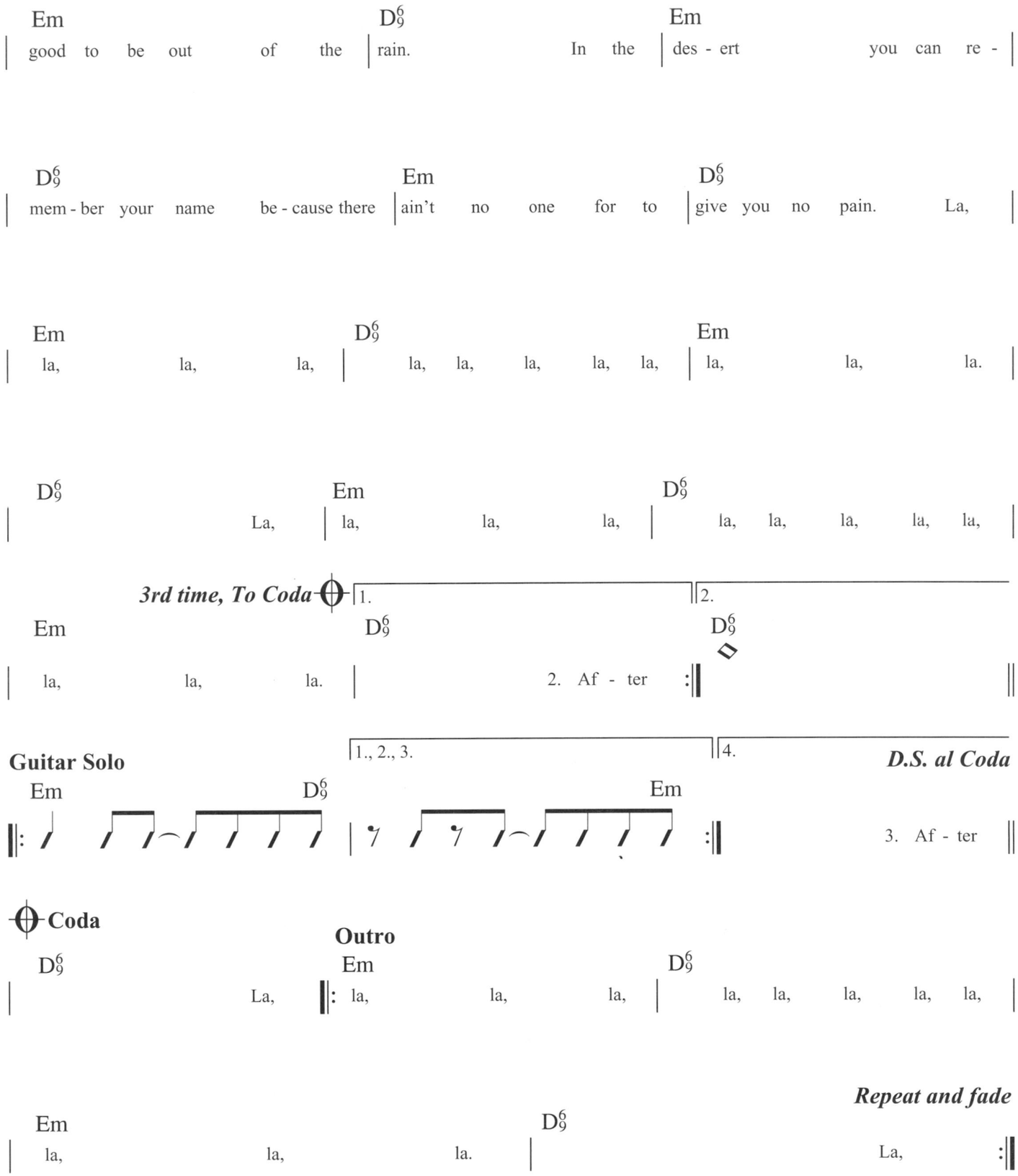

Additional Lyrics

3. After nine days I let the horse run free
'Cause the desert had turned to sea.
There were plants and birds and rocks and things.
There was sand and hills and rains.
The ocean is a desert with its life underground
And the perfect disguise above.
Under the cities lies a heart made of ground,
But the humans will give no love.
You see I've…

I Won't Give Up

Words and Music by Jason Mraz and Michael Natter

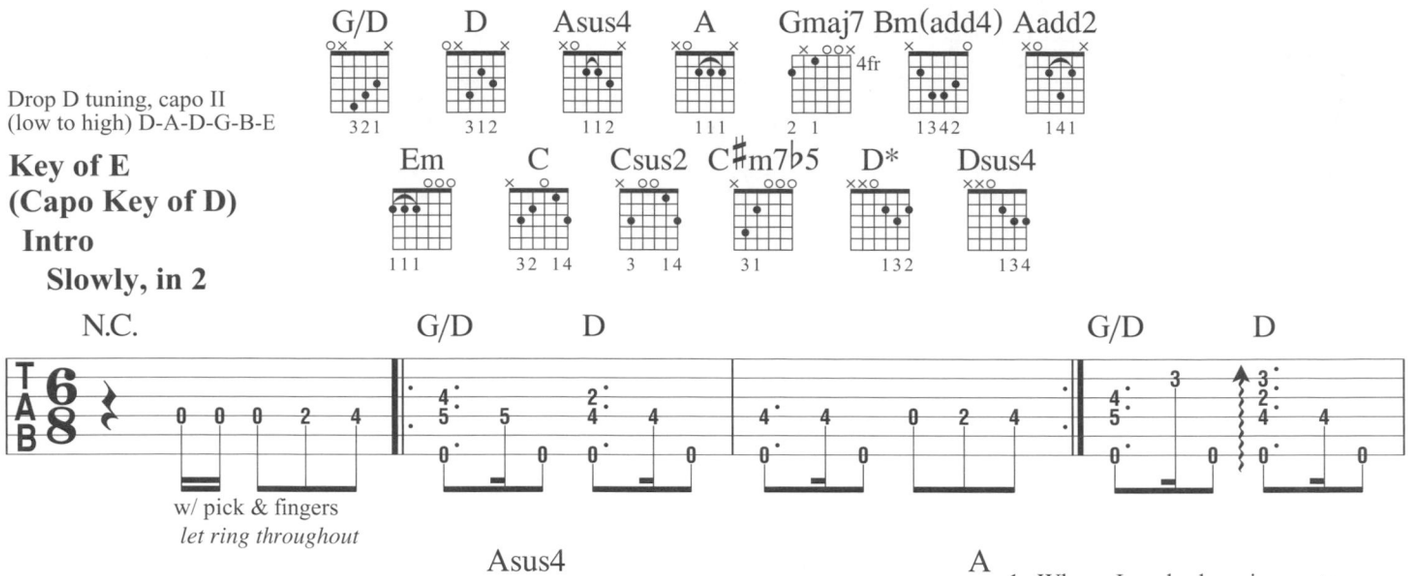

Drop D tuning, capo II
(low to high) D-A-D-G-B-E

Key of E
(Capo Key of D)
Intro
Slowly, in 2

Verse

G/D D G/D D
etc.
your eyes, it's like watch - ing the night sky
old stars, I see that you've come so far
your space to do some - nav - i - gat - ing

G/D D
or a beau - ti - ful sun - rise. Oh, there's so much they
to be right where you are. How old is your
I'll be here pa - tient - ly wait - ing to see what you

Asus4 A A
hold. 2. And just like them Well, I won't give
soul? 'Cause e - ven the
find.

Chorus

Gmaj7 D Bm(add4)
etc.
up on us e - ven if the skies get
stars they burn; some e - ven fall to the

Aadd2 Gmaj7 D
rough. I'm giv - ing you all my love. I'm still look - ing up.
earth. We got a lot to learn. God knows, we're worth

To Coda 1 ⊕

Asus4 A
it.

D.S. al Coda 1
(take 2nd ending)

3. And when you're need - ing

Copyright © 2012 Goo Eyed Music (ASCAP) and Great Hooks Music c/o No BS Publishing (ASCAP)
International Copyright Secured All Rights Reserved

Coda 1

A | Gmaj7
No, I won't give up. | I don't ||

Bridge

Em
||: wan - na be some-one who walks a - way so eas - i - | ly. I'm here to stay and make the dif - fer - ence that |
dif - f'renc - es, they do a lot to teach us how to | use the tools and gifts we got; yeah, we got a |

1. | 2.

A | Asus4 | A | Asus4 | A
I can make. | Our :|| And in the |
lot at stake.

C | Csus2 | C | Csus2
end, you're still my friend; at least we did in - tend for | us to work. We did - n't break; we did - n't burn. |

C♯m7♭5 | C | Csus2
We had to learn how to bend | with - out the world cav - ing in. | I had to learn what I got |

C♯m7♭5 | N.C. | D* | Dsus4 | D*
and what I'm not and who I | am. | I won't give ||

Chorus

Gmaj7 | D | Bm(add4) | Aadd2
||: (3.) up on | us e - ven if the | skies get | rough. I'm giv - ing you |
up on | us. God knows, I'm | tough e - | nough. We've got a |

3rd time, To Coda 2 1.

Gmaj7 | D | Bm(add4)
all my | love. I'm still look - ing up. | I'm still look - ing up. |
lot to | learn. God knows, we're worth

2.

Aadd2 | Asus4 | A
Well, I won't give :|| it. | I won't give ||

D.S.S. al Coda 2

Coda 2

Asus4

Into the Mystic

Words and Music by Van Morrison

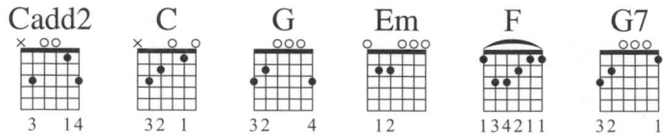

Capo III

Key of E♭ (Capo Key of C)

Intro

Moderately slow

Verse

*C

etc.

1. We were born be - fore the wind. Al - so young - er than the sun.
2. Hark, now hear the sail - ors cry. Smell the sea and feel the sky.

*Chord symbols reflect basic harmony.

G

Ere the bon - nie boat was won as we sailed in - to the mys - tic.
Let your soul and spir - it fly in - to the mys - tic.

C

1. 2.

Pre-Chorus

2nd time, w/ Lead voc. ad lib.

Em F C

And when that fog horn blows I will be com - in' home.

Em F

Yeah, when the fog horn blows I wan - na

© 1970 (Renewed) WB MUSIC CORP. and CALEDONIA SOUL MUSIC
All Rights Administered by WB MUSIC CORP.
All Rights Reserved Used by Permission

G G7

hear it, I don't have to fear it and I

Chorus

C

wan - na rock your gyp - sy soul just like way back

in the days of old. G And mag - nif - i - cent - ly we will float in - to the
And to - geth - er we will flow in - to the

C

mys - tic.
mys - tic. C' - mon girl.

Instrumental

C

G C 1. :

2. G C

Too late to stop now.

Layla

Words and Music by Eric Clapton and Jim Gordon

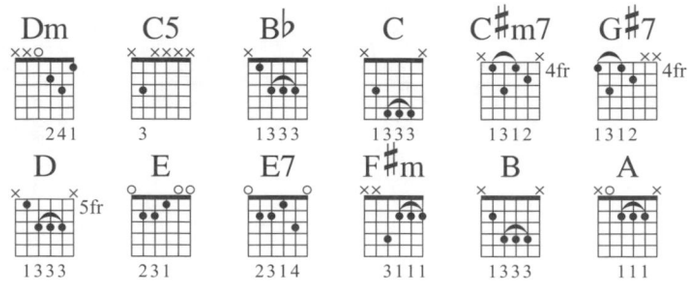

Key of Dm

Intro

Moderately slow (♩♩ = ♩♪)

1. - 5. | 6.

Dm C5 B♭ C Dm N.C.(A) (C)

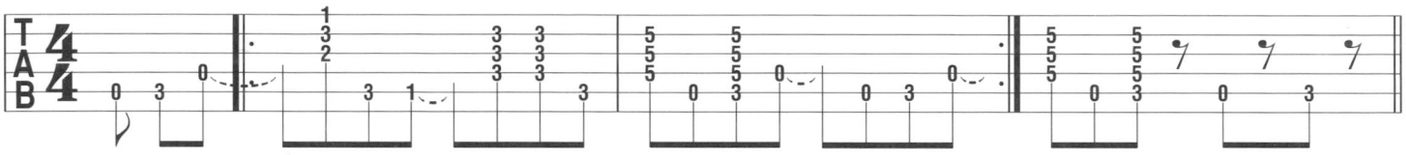

Verse

C♯m7 G♯7

1. What will you do when you get lone - ly?
2. Tried to give you con - sol - a - tion,
3. Make the best of the sit - u - a - tion,

C♯m7 C D E E7 F♯m B

No one wait - ing by your side.
your old man had let you down.
be-fore I fi - n'lly go in - sane.

You've been run - nin',
Like a fool, I
Please don't say we'll

E A F♯m B E A

hid - in' much too long.
fell in love with you.
nev - er find a way,

You know it's just your fool - ish pride.
You turned my whole world up - side down.
tell me all my love's in vain.

Lay - la,

𝄋 Chorus

w/ Intro pattern sim.

Dm C5 B♭ C Dm C5 B♭ C

got me on my knees. Lay - la,

Copyright © 1970 by Eric Patrick Clapton
Copyright Renewed
International Copyright Secured All Rights Reserved

Dm C5 B♭ C Dm

beg - gin' dar - lin' please. Lay - la, dar - lin', won't you ease my wor - ried

1., 2. 3.

C5 B♭ C N.C.(A) (C) Dm

mind? Lay -

C5 B♭ C Dm C5 B♭ C

la, got me on my knees. Lay - la,

To Coda

Dm C5 B♭ C

beg - gin' dar - lin' please. Lay - la,

Dm C5 B♭ C Dm

dar - lin', won't you ease my wor - ried mind?

1. - 7. 8.

Guitar Solo ***D.S. al Coda (take 3rd ending)***

Dm C5 B♭ C Dm Dm

Lay - la,

Coda **Freely** (♩♩ = ♩♩)

C B♭ C Dm

dar - lin', won't you ease my wor - ried mind?

Let Her Go

Words and Music by Michael David Rosenberg

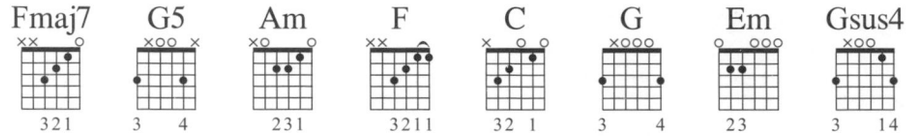

Capo VII

Key of C (Capo Key of G)

Intro

Slow

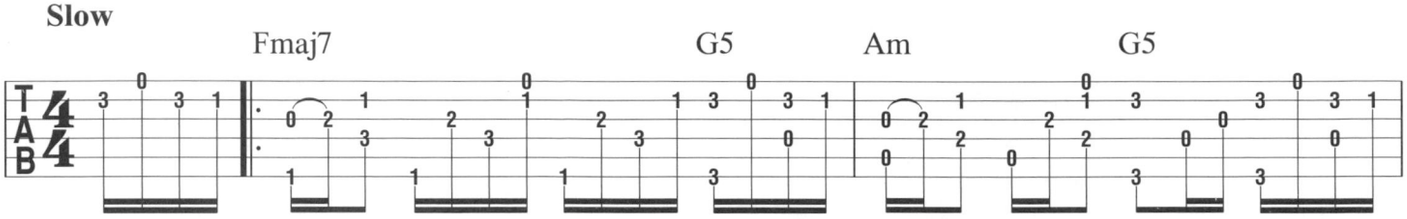

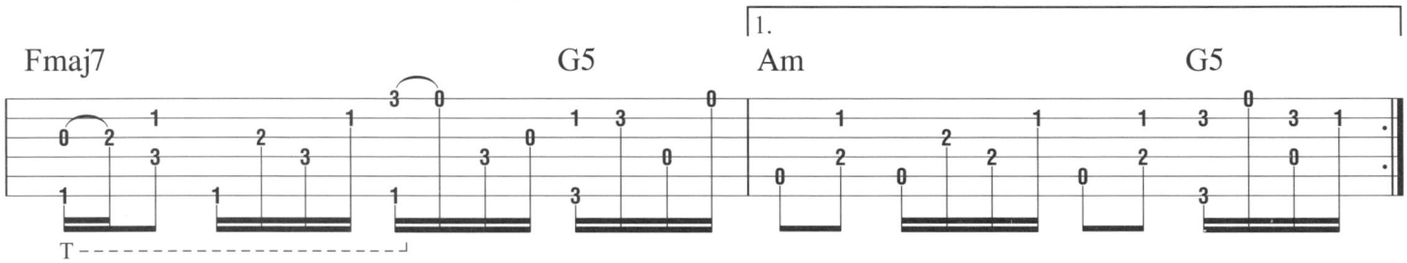

2.

Am G5 F C

Well, you on-ly need the light when it's burn-ing low. On-ly miss the
high when you're feel-ing low. On-ly hate the

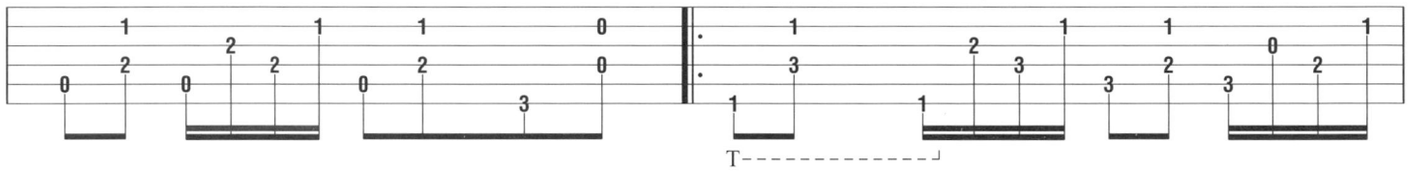

Chorus

G Am F C

etc.

sun when it starts to snow. On-ly know you | love her when you let her go.
road when you're miss-ing home. On-ly know you | love her when you let her go.

1. G

On-ly know you've been :‖

2. **G

And you let her go. ‖

**Let chord ring.

Interlude

Am Fmaj7 G Em Am Fmaj7 G Gsus4 G

Verse

Am Fmaj7 G Em

‖: 1. Star-ing at the bot-tom of your glass, hop-ing one | day you'll make a dream last. But dreams come slow |
2. Star-ing at the ceil-ing in the dark. Same old emp | - ty feel - ing in your heart, 'cause love comes slow |

Copyright © 2012 Sony/ATV Music Publishing (UK) Limited
All Rights Administered by Sony/ATV Music Publishing LLC, 424 Church Street, Suite 1200, Nashville, TN 37219
International Copyright Secured All Rights Reserved

Am Fmaj7 G Gsus4 G

and they go so fast. You
and it goes so fast. Well, you

Am Fmaj7 G Em

see her when you close your eyes. May-be one day you'll un-der-stand why ev - 'ry-thing you
see her when you fall a - sleep. But nev - er to touch and nev - er to keep 'cause you loved her too

Am Fmaj7 G Gsus4 G

touch sure - ly dies. But / Well, you on - ly need the
much and you dived too deep.

𝄋 Chorus

*Fmaj7 C G Am

light when it's burn-ing low. On - ly miss the sun when it starts to snow. On - ly know you

*4th time, let chords ring.

Fmaj7 C G **Gsus4 G

love her when you let her go. On - ly know you've been

**4th time, N.C. till end.

Fmaj7 C G Am

high when you're feel-ing low. On - ly hate the road when you're miss-ing home. On - ly know you

3rd time, To Coda 1

4th time, To Coda 2

1. 2.

Fmaj7 C G Gsus4 G G Gsus4 G

love her when you let her go. :‖ And you let her go, ‖

Bridge

Am Fmaj7 G Gsus4 G Am Fmaj7

oh, oh, oh, no. And you let her go, oh, oh, oh,

G Gsus4 G Am Fmaj7 G Em

no. Well, you let her go.

D.S. al Coda 1

Am Fmaj7 G Gsus4 G

'Cause you on - ly need the ‖

Coda 1 — *D.S. al Coda 2* — Coda 2

G Gsus4 G

'Cause you on - ly need the ‖ And you let her go. ‖

Malagueña

from the Spanish Suite ANDALUCIA
Music and Spanish Lyric by Ernesto Lecuona
English Lyric by Marian Banks

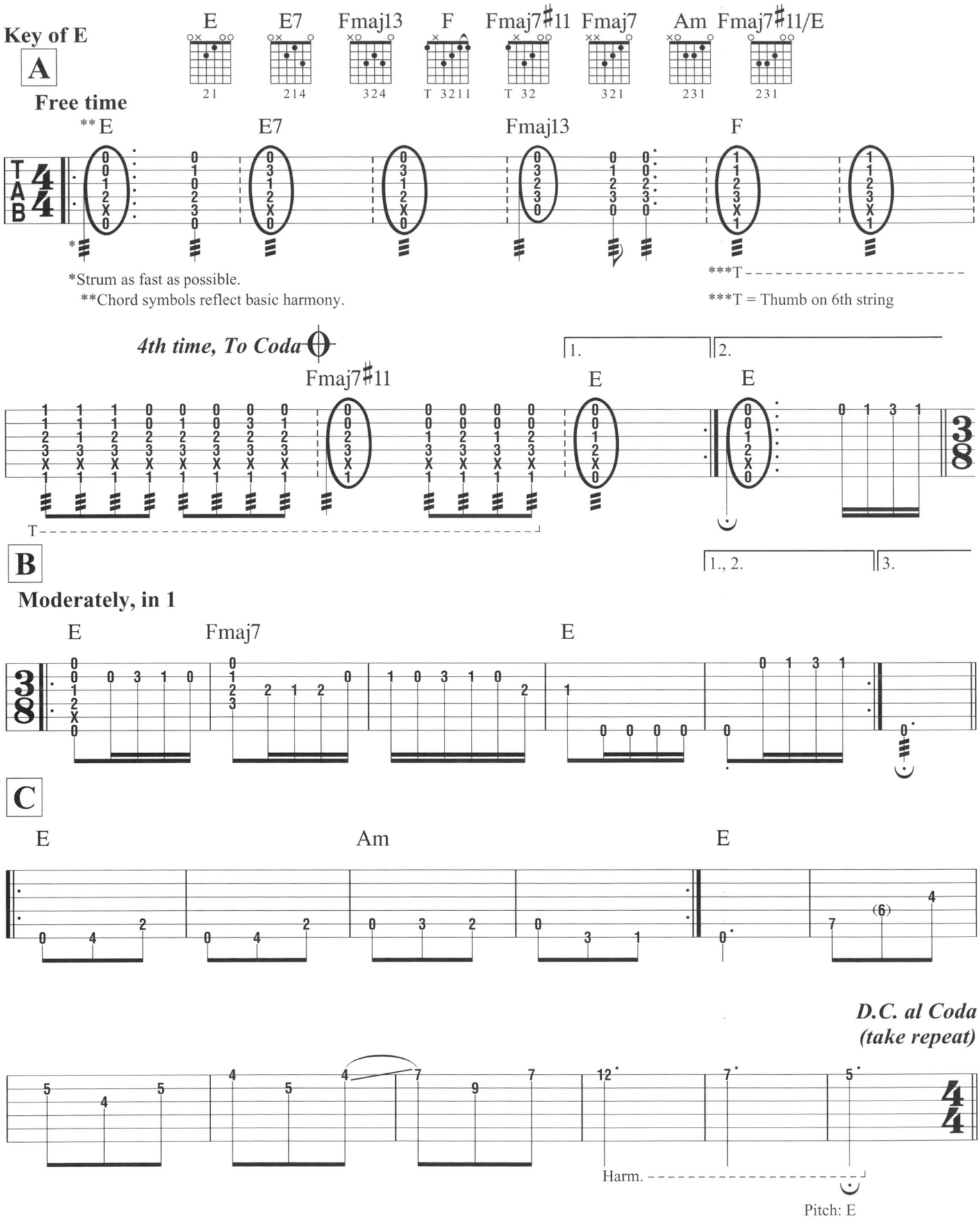

Copyright © 1928 by Edward B. Marks Music Company
Copyright Renewed
International Copyright Secured All Rights Reserved
Used by Permission

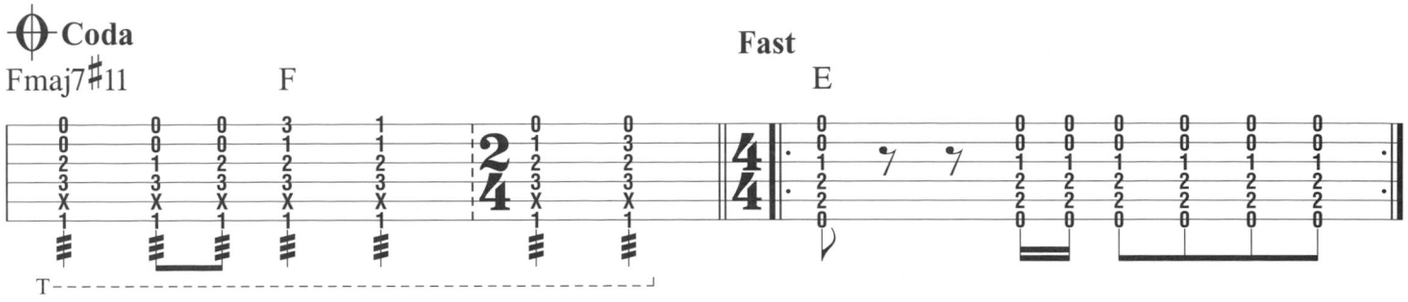

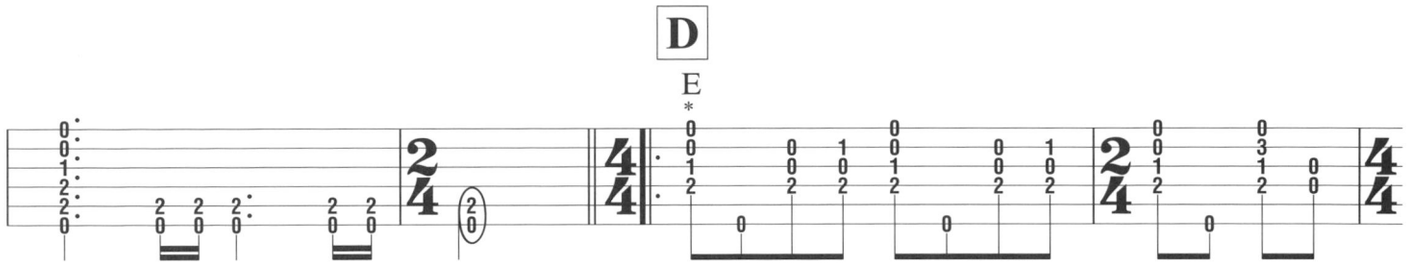

*2nd & 3rd times, no palm mute.

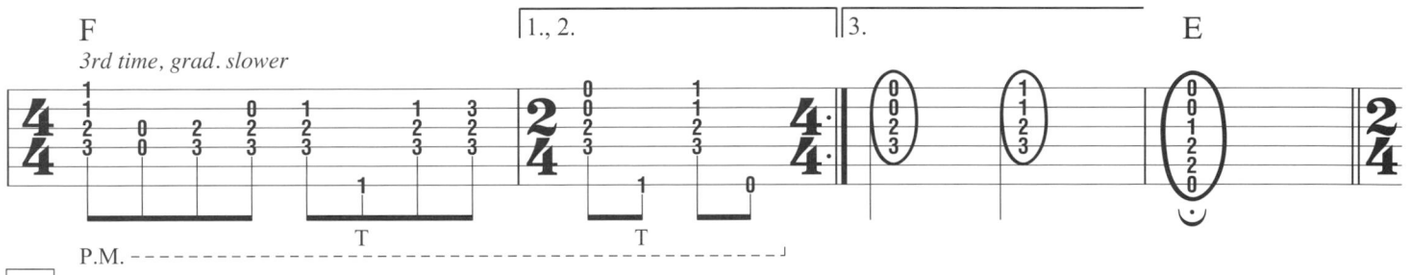

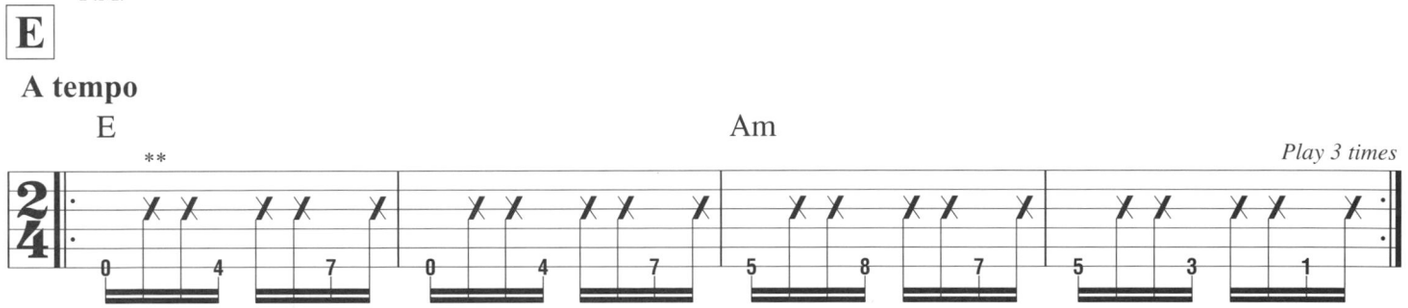

**Slap strings w/ pick hand knuckles.

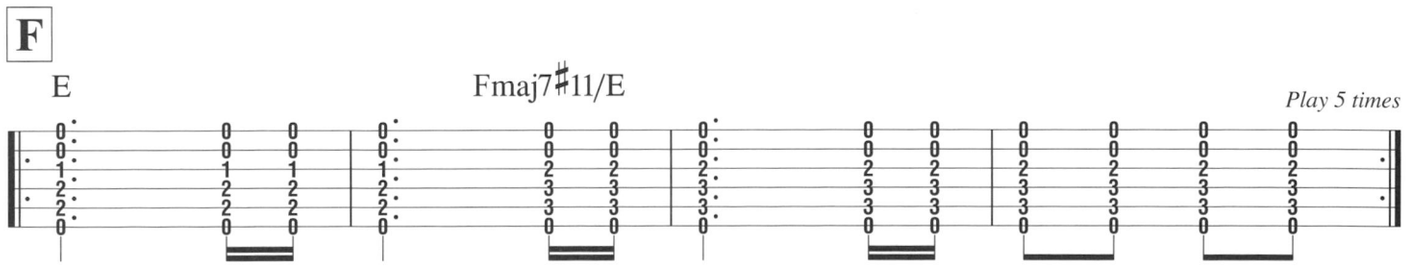

Me and Julio Down by the Schoolyard

Words and Music by Paul Simon

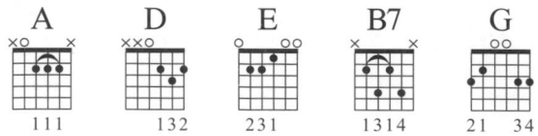

Key of A

Intro

Moderately

A D A E A D A E

Play 3 times

etc.

1. The

Verse

A

ma - ma pa - ja - ma rolled out of bed, and she ran to the po - lice sta -

D E

- tion. When the pa - pa found out he be - gan to shout and we start-

A

- ed the in - ves - ti - ga - tion. It's a - gainst the law,

Interlude

E A

it was a - gainst the law. Oh, what the ma - ma saw,

E A

it was a - gainst the law. 2. Hoo,

𝄋 Verse

A

Ma - ma look down and spit on the ground ev - 'ry time my name gets men -
cou - ple of days they come and take me a - way, but the press let the sto - ry leak.

D E

- tioned. Pa - pa said, "Oy, if I get that boy, I'm gon - na
Now, when the rad - i - cal priest come to get me re - leased, we was

Copyright © 1971 Paul Simon (BMI)
International Copyright Secured All Rights Reserved
Reprinted by Permission

Chorus

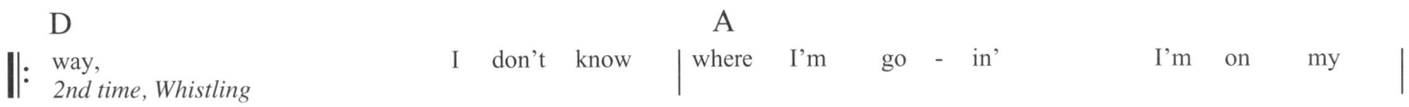

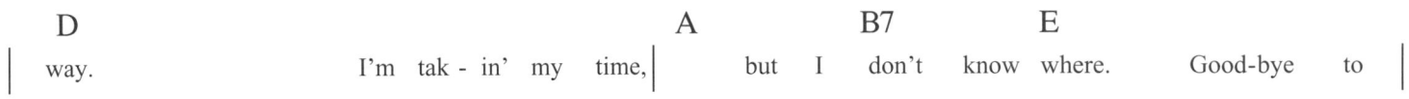

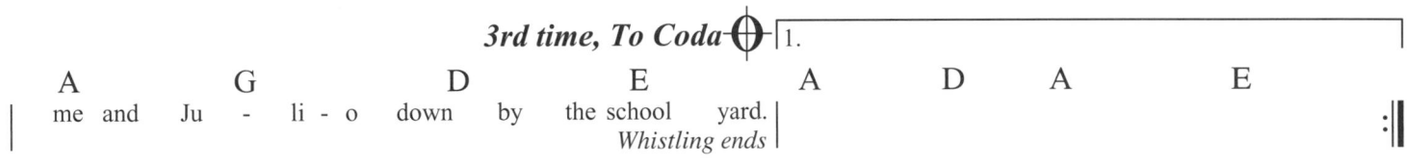

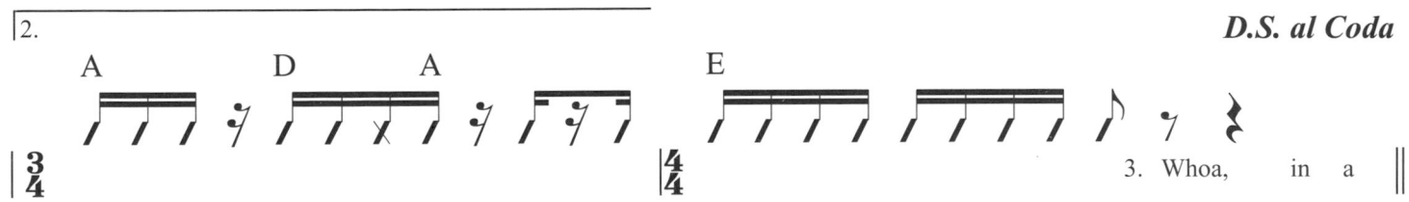

Coda

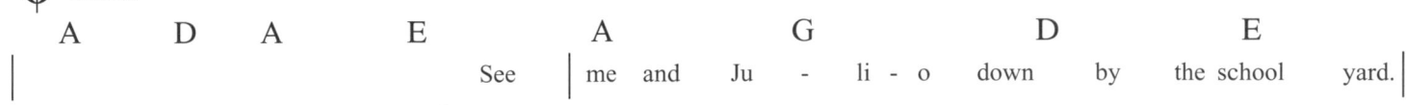

Outro ***Repeat and fade***

Mean

Words and Music by Taylor Swift

Key of E
Verse
Fast

C♯m7 (4fr) 134 | Badd4 1234 | A 234 | E 231 | D 132 | Asus2 23

C♯m7 Badd4 A

etc.

1. You, with your words like knives and swords and weap-ons that you use a - gainst me,
2. You, with your switch-ing sides and your wild - fire lies and your hu - mil - i - a - tion,

C♯m7 Badd4 A

you have knocked me off my feet a - gain, got me feel-ing like a noth - ing.
you, have point - ed out my flaws a - gain, as if I don't al-read-y see them.

C♯m7 Badd4 A

You, with your voice like nails on a chalk-board, call-ing me out when I'm wound-ed.
I walk with my head down, tryin' to block you out 'cause I'll nev-er im-press you,

C♯m7 Badd4 A

You, pick-ing on the weak-er man.
I just wan-na feel o - kay a - gain.

Pre-Chorus

Badd4 E A

Well, you can take me down with just one sin - gle blow.
I bet you got pushed a - round, some - bod-y made you cold.

Badd4 A

To Chorus

But you don't know, what you don't know.
But the cy-cle ends right now, 'cause

2.
A

you can't lead me down that road and you don't know what you don't know.

𝄋 Chorus

*E Badd4 C♯m7 A

Some - day, I'll be liv-in' in a big ol' cit - y and

*3rd time, strum muted strings (next 8 meas.)

E Badd4 A

all you're ev-er gon-na be is mean.

Copyright © 2010 Sony/ATV Music Publishing LLC and Taylor Swift Music
All Rights Administered by Sony/ATV Music Publishing LLC, 424 Church Street, Suite 1200, Nashville, TN 37219
International Copyright Secured All Rights Reserved

E | Badd4 | C♯m7 | A

Some - day, | I'll be | big e-nough so you can't | hit me and |

3rd time, To Coda 1 ⊕ *4th time, To Coda 2* ⊕

E | Badd4 | A

all you're | ev - er gon - na be is | mean. | Why you got - ta be so ||

Interlude

1. | 2.

E | D E | Badd4

mean? | | | :||

Mandolin Solo

Asus2 | Badd4 | Asus2

| | | And I can ||

Bridge

Badd4 | E | A

||: see you years from now | in a bar, | talk-ing o - ver a | foot - ball game, :||
with that same big | loud o - pin - ion but | no - bod-y's | lis - ten - ing.

Badd4 | C♯m7 | Badd4

Washed up and rant | - ing a - bout the | same old | bit - ter |

Asus2 | Badd4

things. | | Drunk and grum - blin' on | a - bout how |

C♯m7 | Badd4 | Asus2

I can't | sing. | But all you are is ||

Interlude

E | Badd4 | C♯m7 | A

mean. | | | All you are is ||

E | Badd4 | C♯m7

||: mean and a | li - ar and pa - | thet - ic and a - |
mean, and | mean, and | mean, and

2nd time, D.S. al Coda 1 ⊕ **Coda 1** *D.S. al Coda 2* ⊕ **Coda 2**

A | E

lone in life and :|| | Why you got - ta be so... || | mean? | ||
mean. But...

Melissa

Words and Music by Gregg Allman and Steve Alaimo

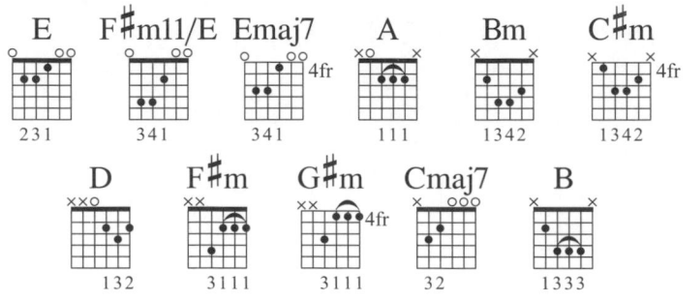

Key of E

Intro

Moderately slow

E F♯m7/E Emaj7

etc.

Verse

F♯m7/E E F♯m7/E

1. Cross - roads seem to come and
2. Freight train, each car looks the
3. Cross - roads, will you ev - er let him

Emaj7 F♯m7/E E

go, yeah. The gyp - sy flies from coast to coast,
same, all the same. And no one knows the gyp - sy's name.
go, no, no, no, or will you hide the dead man's

F♯m7/E A Bm C♯m D

ghost? know - in' man - y, lov - in' none,
No one hears his lone - ly sigh.
Lord, or will he lie be - neath the plain,

E F♯m G♯m A Cmaj7

bear-ing sor - row, hav - ing fun, but back home he'll al - ways
There are no blan - kets where he's ly - in', Lord, but in the deep - est dreams, the gyp - sy flies
or will his spir-it fall a - way? But I know that he won't

Copyright © 1968 by Unichappell Music Inc., EMI Longitude Music and Elijah Blue Music
Copyright Renewed
International Copyright Secured All Rights Reserved

3rd time, To Coda

B | E | F♯m7/E

run to sweet Mel - is | - sa, | Hmm.
with sweet Mel - is | - sa.
stay with - out Mel - is - sa.

Bridge

Emaj7 | F♯m7/E | E

(1.) Hmm, mm. | :‖ A - gain the morn - in's come,

D | A

a - gain he's on the run. | Sun - beams shin - in' through his hair.

B | C♯m

Bet - ter not to have a care, | so pick up your gear and, gyp - sy, roll

D.S. al Coda

A | B

on. | Roll on. | ‖

Coda

Cmaj7 | B | E

Yes, I know that he won't | stay, yeah, with - out Mel - ‖: is - sa.

Outro

w/ Lead Voc. ad lib. on repeats

Repeat and fade

F♯m7/E | Emaj7 | F♯m7/E

No, no, | just won't stay. :‖

More Than a Feeling

Words and Music by Tom Scholz

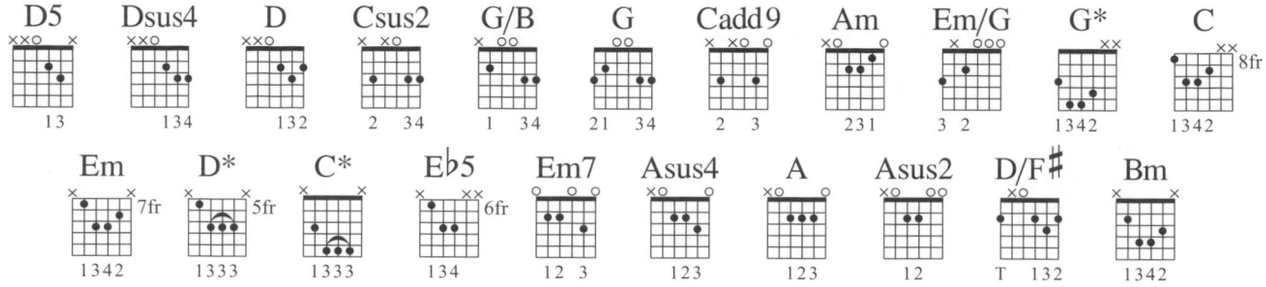

Key of D

Intro

Moderately

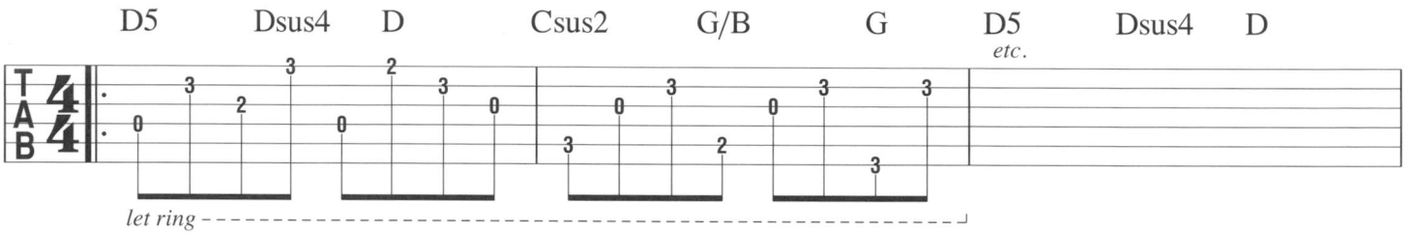

1. Csus2 G/B G Csus2 G/B G :‖

2. 1. I

𝄋 Verse

D5 Dsus4 D

looked out this morn - ing and
2. So man - y peo - ple have
3. When I'm tired and think -

Csus2 G/B G D5 Dsus4 D Csus2 G/B G

the sun was gone, turned on some mu - sic to start my day. I
come and gone, their fac - es fade as the years go by. Yet
ing cold, I hide in my mu - sic, for - get the day and

D5 Dsus4 D Csus2 G/B G D5 Dsus4 D

lost my - self in a fa-mil - iar song. I closed my eyes and I
I still re - call as I wan-der on, as clear as the sun in
dream of a girl I used to know. I closed my eyes and she

Cadd9 G/B Am Em/G D Dsus4

slipped a - way.
the sum-mer sky.
slipped a - way.

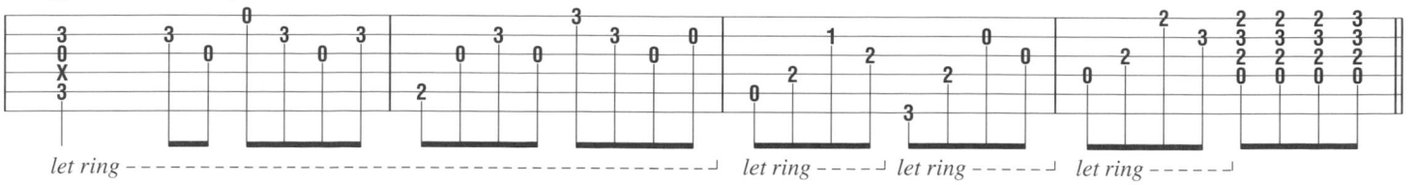

Copyright © 1976 Pure Songs
Copyright Renewed
All Rights Administered by Next Decade Entertainment, Inc.
All Rights Reserved Used by Permission

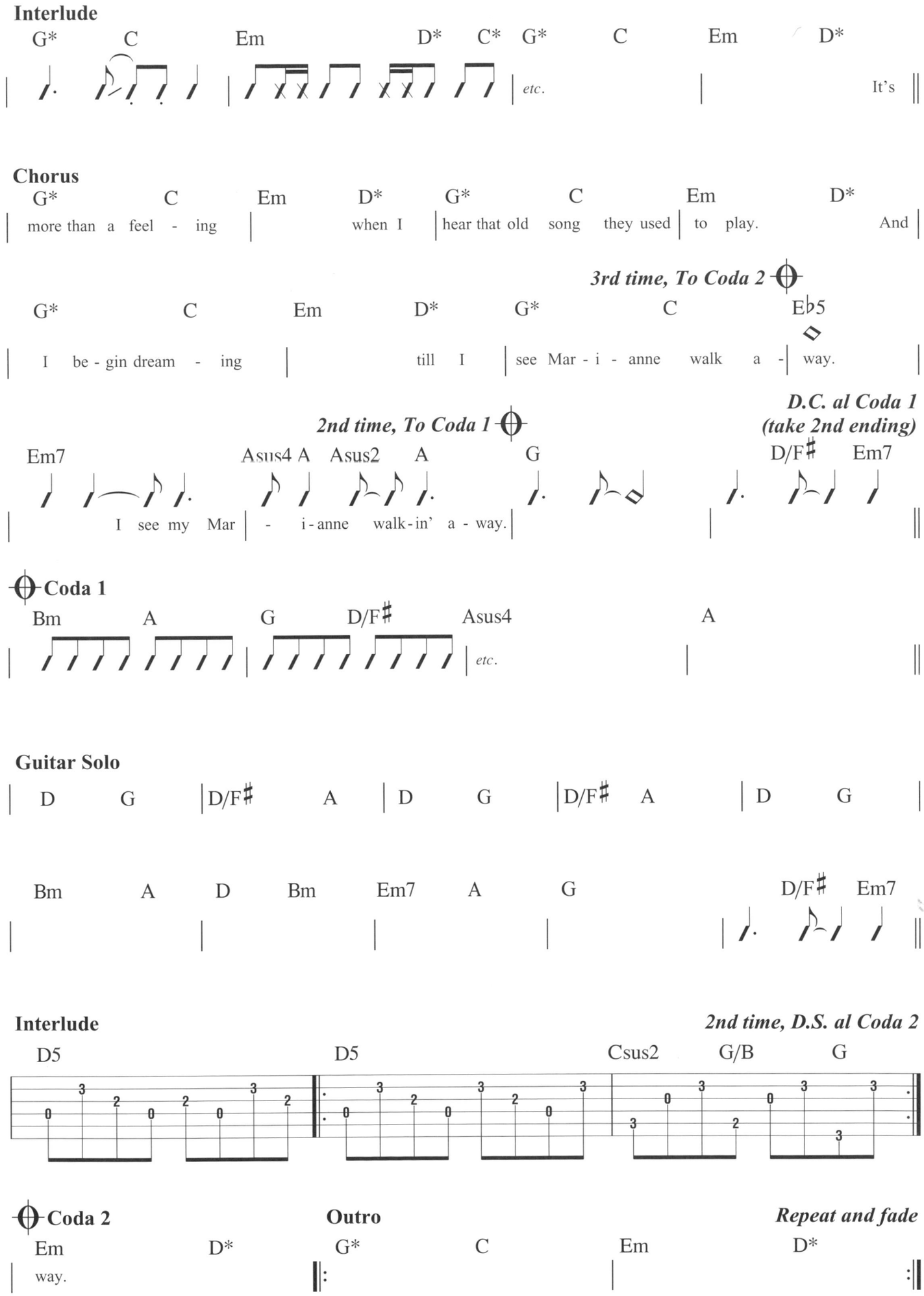
Interlude
G* C Em D* C* G* C Em D*
etc.
It's
Chorus
G* C Em D* G* C Em D*
more than a feel - ing when I hear that old song they used to play. And
3rd time, To Coda 2
G* C Em D* G* C E♭5
I be - gin dream - ing till I see Mar - i - anne walk a - way.
D.C. al Coda 1
(take 2nd ending)
2nd time, To Coda 1
Em7 Asus4 A Asus2 A G D/F♯ Em7
I see my Mar - i - anne walk - in' a - way.
Coda 1
Bm A G D/F♯ Asus4 A
etc.
Guitar Solo
D G D/F♯ A D G D/F♯ A D G
Bm A D Bm Em7 A G D/F♯ Em7
Interlude
2nd time, D.S. al Coda 2
D5 D5 Csus2 G/B G
Coda 2
Outro
Repeat and fade
Em D* G* C Em D*
way.

More Than Words

Words and Music by Nuno Bettencourt and Gary Cherone

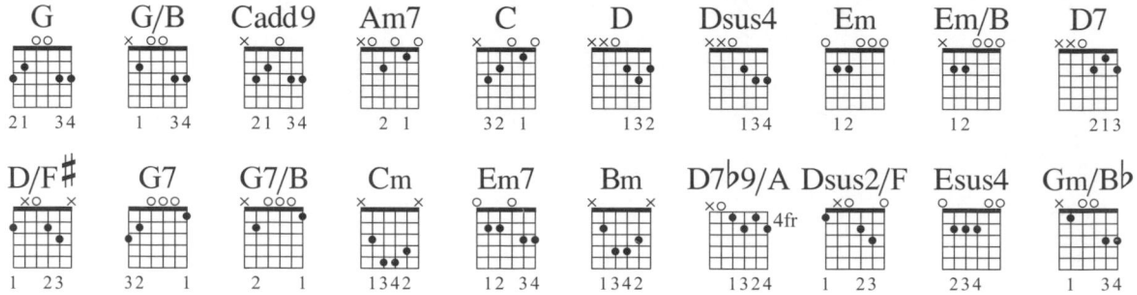

Tune down 1/2 step:
(low to high) E♭-A♭-D♭-G♭-B♭-E♭

Key of G

Intro

Moderately slow

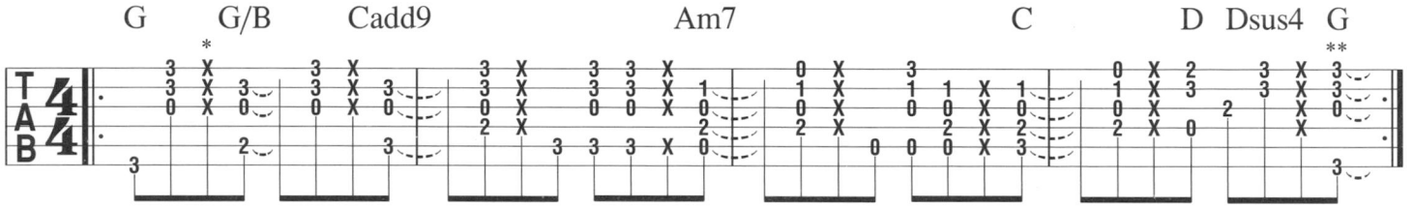

*Hit muted strings w/ R.H. throughout.

**Hold into beat 1 on repeat.

𝄋 Verse

etc.

G G/B Cadd9 Am7 C D Dsus4 G
1. Say - in', "I love you," is not the words I want to hear from you.
2. Now that I've tried to talk to you and make you un - der - stand,

G/B Cadd9 Am7 C D Dsus4 Em
It's not that I want you not to say, but if you on - ly knew
all you have to do is close your eyes and just reach out your hands

Em/B Am7 D7 G D/F♯ Em
how eas - y it would be to show me how you feel.
and touch me. Hold me close, don't ev - er let me go.

Chorus

Em/B Am7 D7 G7
More than words is all you have to do
More than words is all I ev - er need -

G7/B C Cm G
to make it real. Then you would - n't have to say
- ed you to show.

Em7 Am7 D7 ***(D7♭9/A)
◇ ◇
that you love me 'cause I'd al - read - y

***2nd time only

G G/B G G/B D/F♯ Em Bm C
know. What would you do if my heart was torn in two?

Copyright © 1990 COLOR ME BLIND MUSIC
All Rights Administered by ALMO MUSIC CORP.
All Rights Reserved Used by Permission

G/B Am7 D7 G

More than words | to show you feel | that your love | for me is real.

G/B G G/B D/F♯ Em Bm C

What | would you say | if I took | those words a - way?

To Coda ⊕

G/B Am7 D7

Then you could | - n't make things new | just by say | - in', "I love you." ||

Interlude

G G/B Cadd9 Am7 C D Dsus4 G

| (La, dee, da la, dee, da, | dee, dai, dai, da.) | More than words. |

D.S. al Coda

G/B Cadd9 Am7 D7

| (La, dee, da, dai, da.) | | ||

⊕ **Coda**

Interlude

G G/B Cadd9 Am7 C D Dsus4 G

Play 3 times

||: | (La, dee, da la, dee, da, | dee, dai, dai, da.) | More than words. :||

G/B Cadd9 Am7 C D

| (La, dee, da la, dee, da, | la, | da, da...) More than ||

Outro

G D/F♯ Dsus2/F

words. Oo, oo, oo, oo,

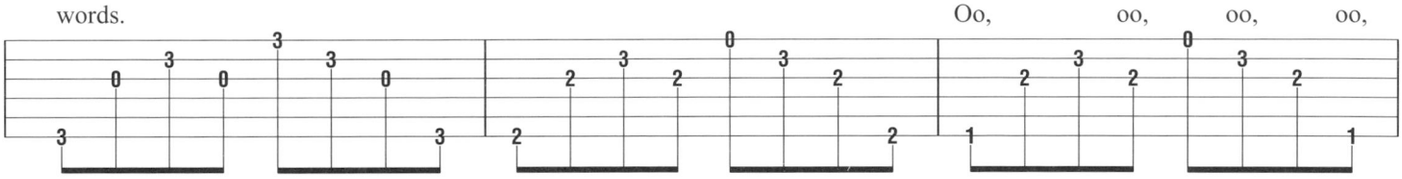

Slower **Freely**

Esus4 Am7 D N.C.

oo, oo, oo. More than

grad. slower *grad. slower*

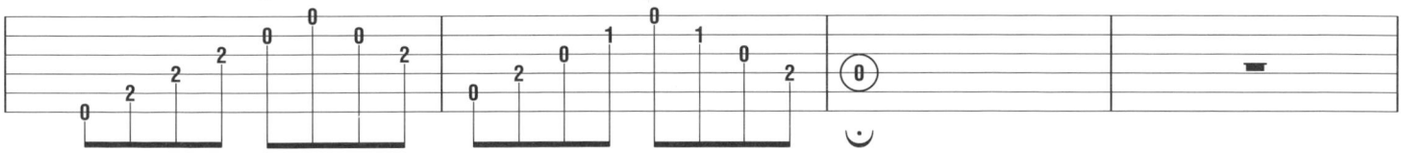

G Cadd9 G/B Gm/B♭ Am7 G

words.

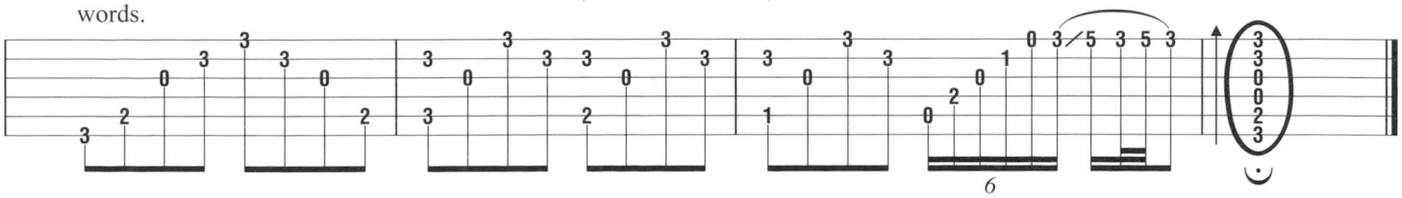

6

Nothing Else Matters

Words and Music by James Hetfield and Lars Ulrich

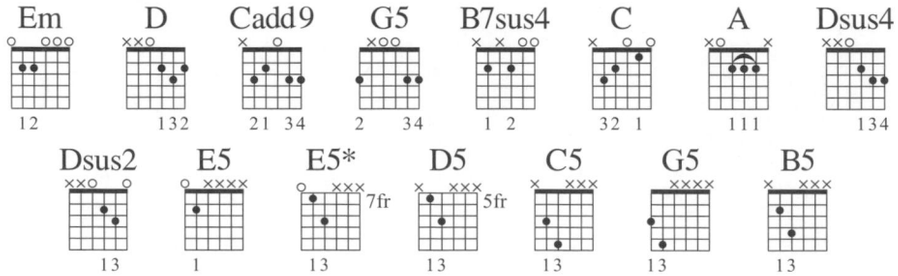

Key of Em

Intro

Slow, in 2

Verse

Em Em D Cadd9

Play 4 times

1., 7. So close, no mat-ter how far.

let ring throughout
w/ fingers

Em D Cadd9 Em

Could-n't be much more from the heart. For-ev-er trust - ing

To Coda 2

D Cadd9 G5 B7sus4 Em

who we are. And noth-ing else mat-ters.

Verse

etc.

Em D Cadd9 Em

2., 5. Nev-er o-pened my - self this way. Life is ours, we live it
3., 6. Trust I seek and I find in you. Ev-'ry day for us
4. So close, no mat-ter how far. Could-n't be much more

D Cadd9 Em D Cadd9

our way. All these words I don't just say.
some-thing new. O-pen mind for a dif-f'rent view.
from the heart. For-ev-er trust - ing who we are.

1. 2.

3rd time, To Coda 1

G5 B7sus4 Em C A

And noth-ing else mat-ters.

Copyright © 1991 Creeping Death Music (ASCAP)
International Copyright Secured All Rights Reserved

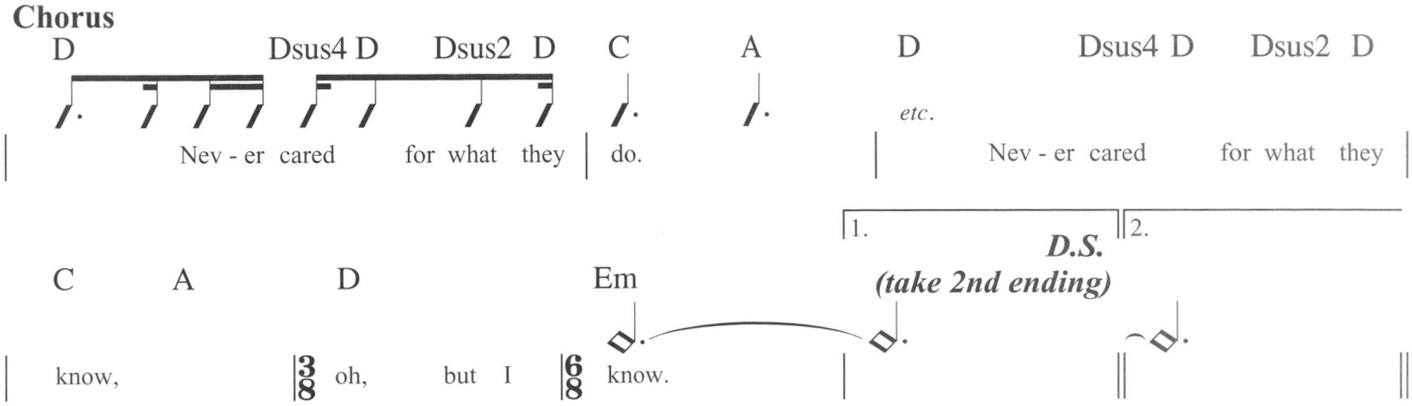
Chorus
D Dsus4 D Dsus2 D C A D Dsus4 D Dsus2 D
Nev - er cared for what they do.
etc.
Nev - er cared for what they
1. 2.
D.S.
(take 2nd ending)
C A D Em
know, oh, but I know.

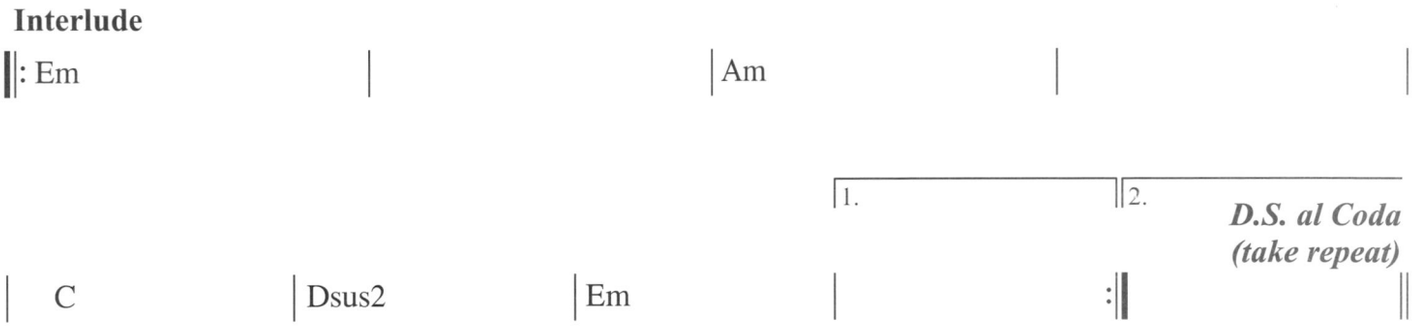
Interlude
Em
Am
1. 2.
D.S. al Coda
(take repeat)
C Dsus2 Em

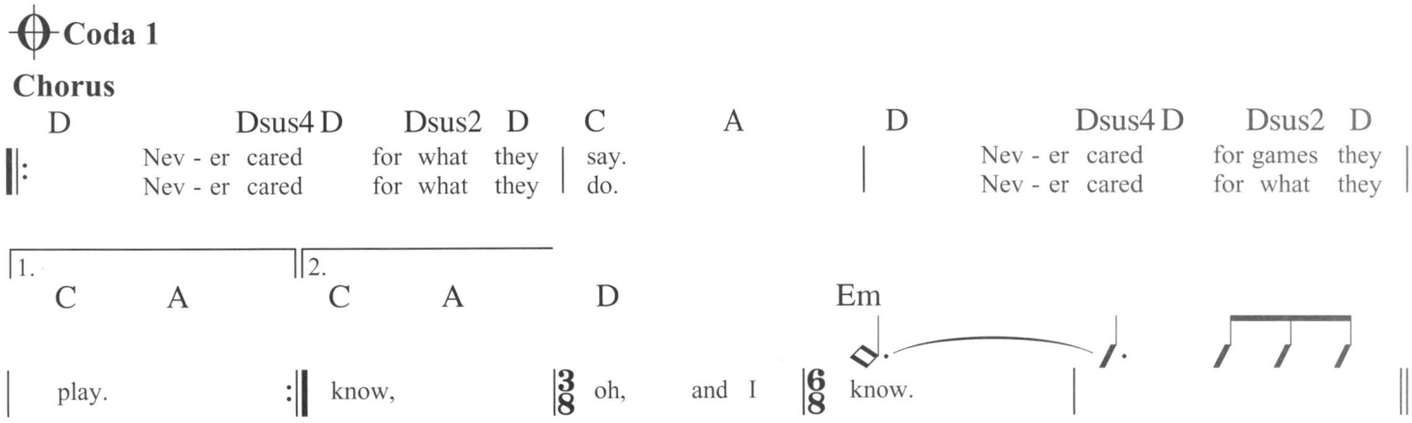
Coda 1
Chorus
D Dsus4 D Dsus2 D C A D Dsus4 D Dsus2 D
Nev - er cared for what they say.
Nev - er cared for what they do.
Nev - er cared for games they
Nev - er cared for what they
1. 2.
C A C A D Em
play. know, oh, and I know.

Guitar Solo
w/ Intro riff
D.S.S. al Coda 2
E5 E5* D5 C5 G5* B5 Em
Play 3 times
4

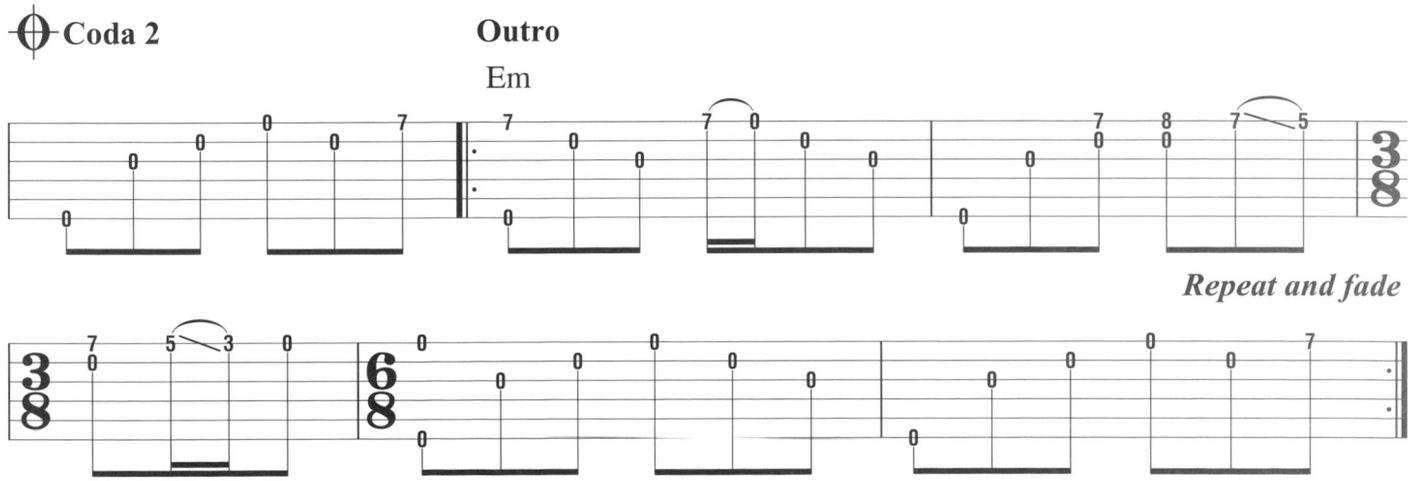
Coda 2
Outro
Em
Repeat and fade

One

Lyrics by Bono and The Edge
Music by U2

Key of C

Intro

Moderately slow (♫ = ♫)

Am | Dsus2 | Fmaj7 | G

P.M. ----------

Verse

Am | Dsus2 | Fmaj7

1. Is it get - ting bet - ter, or do you feel the same?
2. Did I dis - ap - point you or leave a bad taste in your
3. Have you come here for for - give-ness, have you come to raise the

G | Am | Dsus2

mouth? Will it make it eas - i - er on you, now
dead? You act like you've nev - er had love,
Have you come here to play Je - sus

Fmaj7 | G

and you want me to go with - out.
to the lep - ers in your head?
you got some - one to blame? You say
Well, it's

Chorus

C | Am | Fmaj7

one love, one life, when it's one need
too late, to - night, to drag the past out in -
Did I ask too much, more than a lot? You gave me noth - ing, now it's

C | Am

in the night. One love, we get to share it,
- to the light. We're one, but we're not the same, we got to
all I got. We're one, but we're not the same, well, we

Fmaj7 | C

(it) leaves you, ba - by, if you don't care for it.
car - ry each - oth - er, car - ry each - oth - er... one.
hurt each - oth - er, then we do it a - gain. You say

Copyright © 1991 UNIVERSAL - POLYGRAM INTERNATIONAL MUSIC PUBLISHING B.V.
All Rights in the United States and Canada Controlled and Administered by UNIVERSAL - POLYGRAM INTERNATIONAL PUBLISHING, INC.
All Rights Reserved Used by Permission

1., 2.

Interlude

Am | Dsus2 | Fmaj7 | G

etc.

3.

Bridge

C | love is a tem - ple, love | Am | a high - er law, love | C | is a tem - ple, love |

Am | the high - er law. You ask | C | me to en - ter, but | G | then you make me crawl, and |

Fmaj7 | I can't be hold - ing on | to what you've got | when all you've got is hurt. ||

Chorus

C | One love, | Am | one blood, | Fmaj7 | one life, you got to |

C | do what you should. | One life, | Am | with each - oth - er: |

Fmaj7 | sis - ters, | C | broth - ers. | One life but we're |

Am | not the same, we get to | Fmaj7 | car - ry each - oth - er, car - ry | C | each - oth - er. One, ||

Outro

w/ Lead Voc. ad lib. on repeats

C | Am | Fmaj7 | C | *Play 4 times*

one.

Am | Fmaj7 | C

Ah, ah. | Oh, ah, | ah. | Yeah. ||

Patience

Words and Music by W. Axl Rose, Slash, Izzy Stradlin', Duff McKagan and Steven Adler

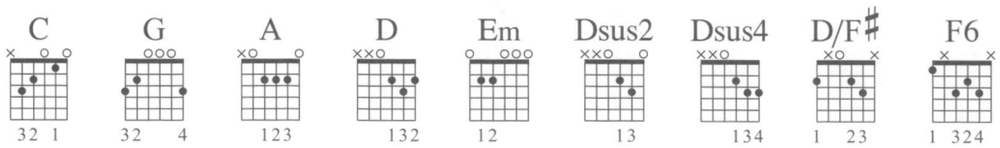

Tune down 1/2 step:
(low to high) E♭-A♭-D♭-G♭-B♭-E♭

Key of G

Intro

Moderately

C G

sim. on repeat

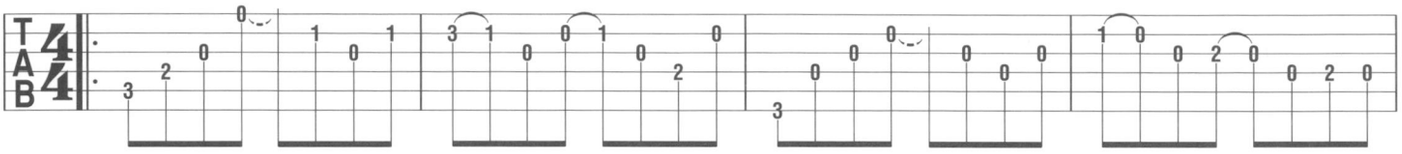

let ring throughout

A D

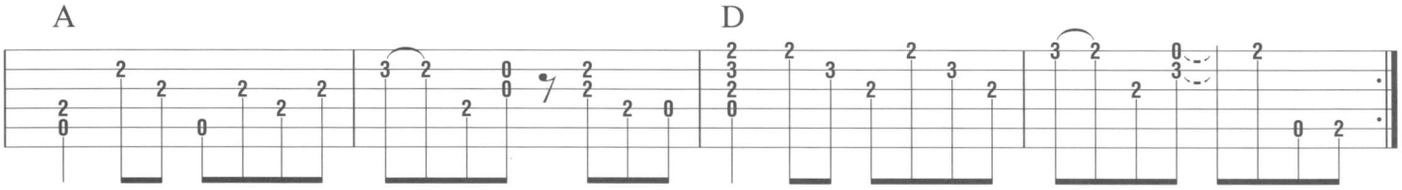

Instrumental Chorus

C G C Em D

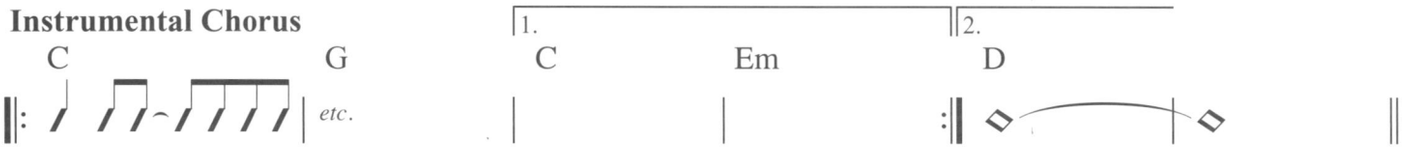

Verse

w/ Intro pattern

C G

1. Shed a tear 'cause I'm | miss-in' you. | I'm still al - right to smile. |
2. I sit here | on the stairs 'cause I'd | rath-er be a - lone. | If |

A D

| Girl, I think a - bout | you ev - 'ry day | now. |
| I can't have you right | now, I'll wait, | dear. |

C G

| Was a time when I | was-n't sure, but you | set my mind at ease. |
| Some - times I | get so tense, but I | can't speed up the time. | But |

A D

| There is no doubt | you're in my heart | now. |
| you know, love there's one | more thing to con-sid | - er. |

𝄋 Chorus

C G C Em

| Said, "Wom-an, | take it slow, it - 'll | work it - self out fine. |
| Said, "Wom-an, | take it slow, and | things will be just fine. |

3rd time, Guitar Solo

Copyright © 1988 Guns N' Roses Music (ASCAP) and Black Frog Music (ASCAP)
All Rights for Black Frog Music in the U.S. and Canada Controlled and Administered by Universal - PolyGram International Publishing, Inc.
International Copyright Secured All Rights Reserved

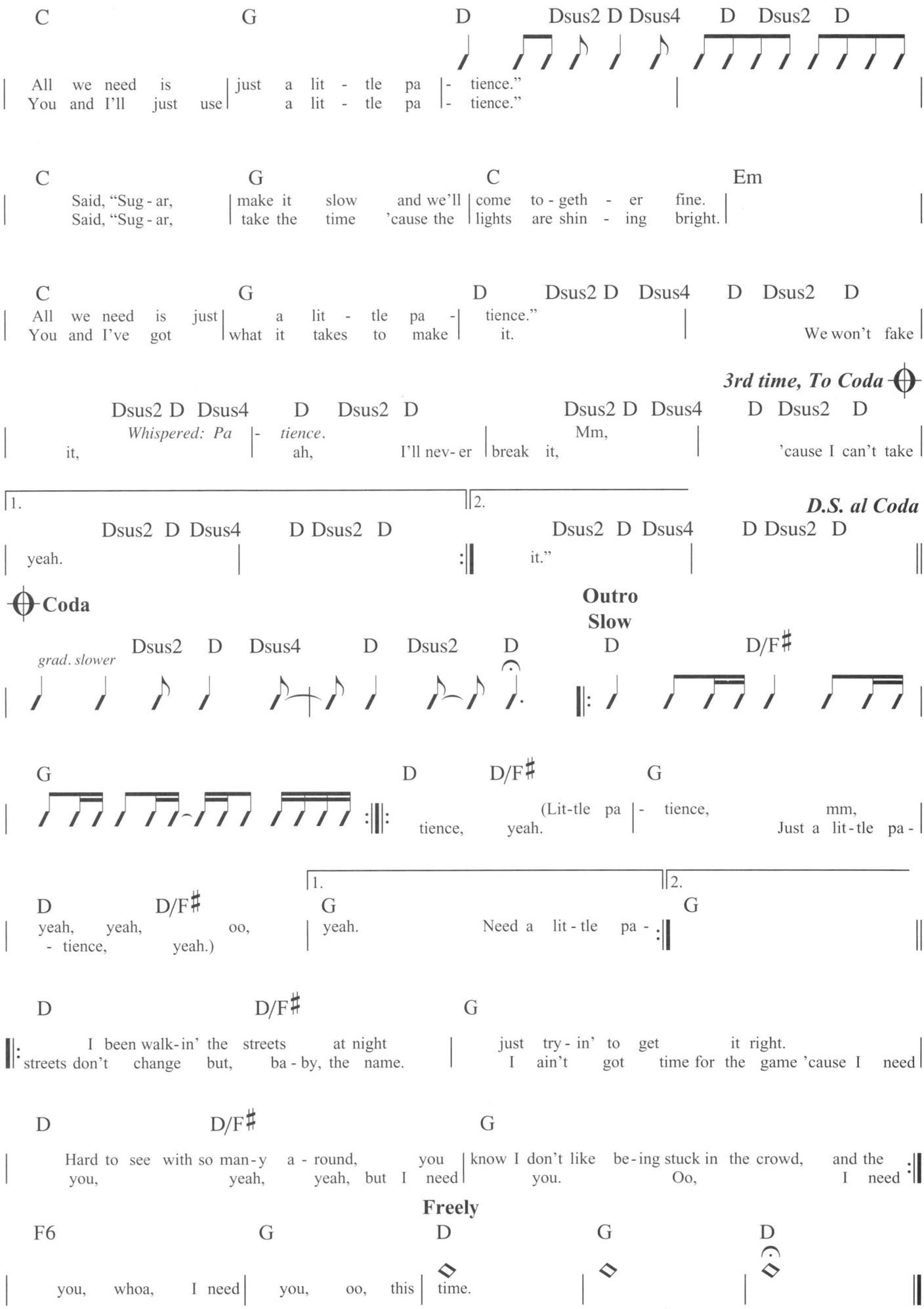
C G D Dsus2 D Dsus4 D Dsus2 D
All we need is just a lit - tle pa - tience."
You and I'll just use a lit - tle pa - tience."
C G C Em
Said, "Sug - ar, make it slow and we'll come to - geth - er fine.
Said, "Sug - ar, take the time 'cause the lights are shin - ing bright.
C G D Dsus2 D Dsus4 D Dsus2 D
All we need is just a lit - tle pa - tience."
You and I've got what it takes to make it. We won't fake
3rd time, To Coda
Dsus2 D Dsus4 D Dsus2 D Dsus2 D Dsus4 D Dsus2 D
Whispered: Pa - tience.
it, ah, I'll nev - er break it, Mm, 'cause I can't take
1.
2.
D.S. al Coda
Dsus2 D Dsus4 D Dsus2 D Dsus2 D Dsus4 D Dsus2 D
yeah. it."
Coda
Outro
Slow
grad. slower
Dsus2 D Dsus4 D Dsus2 D D D/F♯
G D D/F♯ G
tience, yeah. (Lit-tle pa - tience, mm, Just a lit-tle pa -
D D/F♯ G G
yeah, yeah, oo, yeah. Need a lit - tle pa -
- tience, yeah.)
D D/F♯ G
I been walk-in' the streets at night just try - in' to get it right.
streets don't change but, ba - by, the name. I ain't got time for the game 'cause I need
D D/F♯ G
Hard to see with so man - y a - round, you know I don't like be - ing stuck in the crowd, and the
you, yeah, yeah, but I need you. Oo, I need
Freely
F6 G D G D
you, whoa, I need you, oo, this time.

Peaceful Easy Feeling

Words and Music by Jack Tempchin

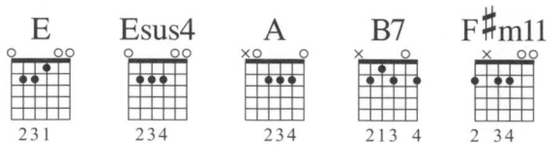

Key of E

Intro

Moderately fast

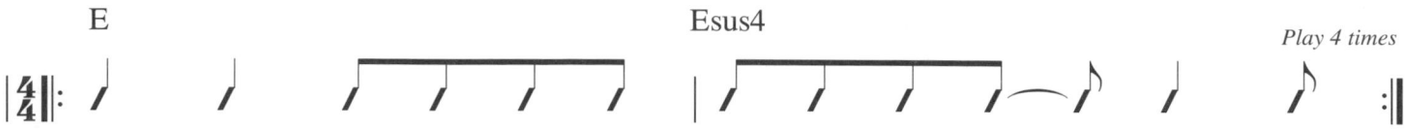

Verse

*E A E A

etc.

1. I like the way | your spark - ling ear | - rings | lay
2. And I found | out a long | time a - go |
3. I get this | feel - in' I may | know you

*3rd time, let chords ring, next 2 meas.

E A B7

a - gainst your | skin so brown. |
what a wom-an can do | to your soul, |
as a lov - er | and a friend,

E A E A

And I wan - na | sleep with you in the | des - ert to - night |
ah, but she | can't take you | an - y - way |
but this voice keeps | whis - per - ing in my oth - er ear, tells me

E A B7

with a bil - lion | stars all a - round. | 'Cause I got a
you don't al-read-y know | how to go. | And I got a
I may nev - er | see you a - gain. | 'Cause I get a

Chorus

A E

peace - ful | eas - y feel | - ing, |

A F♯m11 B7

and I know you won't | let me down, | 'cause I'm

3rd time, To Coda

E F♯m11 A B7

al - | read - y stand | - ing | on the ground. |

© 1972 (Renewed) WB MUSIC CORP. and JAZZ BIRD MUSIC
All Rights Administered by WB MUSIC CORP.
All Rights Reserved Used by Permission

| E | Esus4 | E | Esus4 :‖

Guitar Solo

‖: E | A | E | A |

| E | A | B7 | | :‖

| A | | E | | |

| A | | B7 | | |

D.S. al Coda

| E | F♯m11 | A | B7 ‖

Coda

B7 E F♯m11 A B7

| I'm | al - | read-y | stand - ing. | Yes, I'm |

E F♯m11 A B7

| al - | read - y | stand - ing | on the ground. ‖

Outro

E F♯m11 A B7 E

Play 3 times

‖: | | | :‖ ‖

Redemption Song

Words and Music by Bob Marley

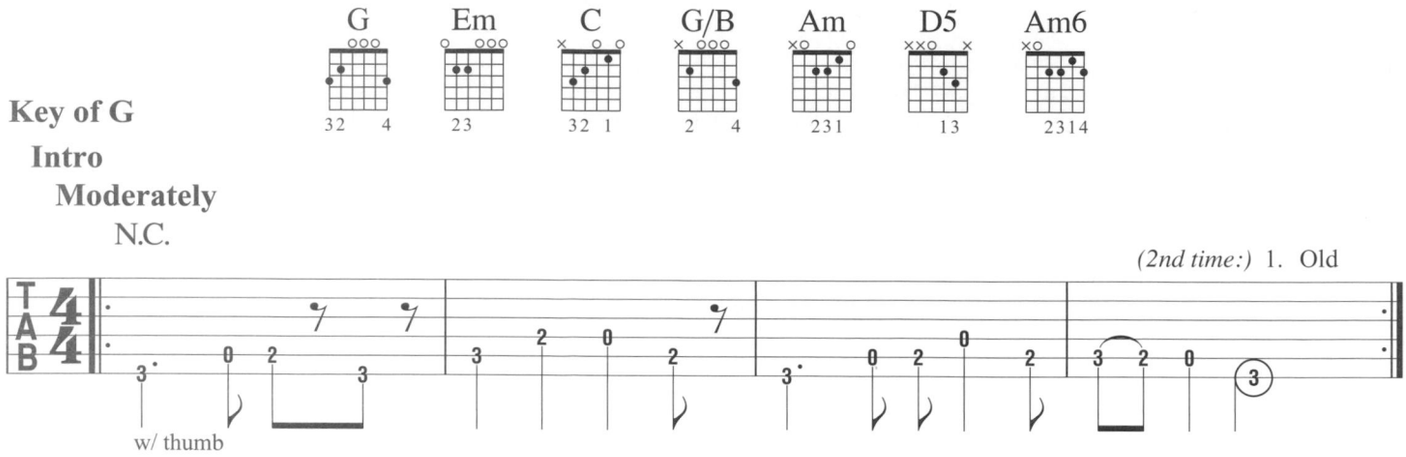

Verse

G Em C G/B

|: pi - rates, yes, they rob | I, sold | I to the mer-chant ships |
(3.) pate your - selves from men - tal | slav - 'ry. None but our | - selves can free our minds. |

Am G Em

etc.

| Have no | fear for min - utes af - ter they took a - tom - ic en - | I er - gy 'cause none of |

C G/B *Am G

| them from can the stop bot - tom the - less time. | pit. But my How long | hand shall was made they kill our proph - |

*2nd & 3rd times, substitute D5.

Em C G/B Am

| - strong - ets while we | stand by the a - hand side of the and Al - look? | might - y. Oo. We Some for - |

G Em C **(G/B)

| say - ward it's in just this a part gen - er - | of a - it, tion, we've got | to tri ful - um - fill phant - the Book. |

**2nd & 3rd times only.

Chorus

D5 G

| - ly. } | Won't you help to sing ‖ |

Copyright © 1980 Fifty-Six Hope Road Music Ltd. and Odnil Music Ltd.
All Rights in North America Administered by Blue Mountain Music Ltd./
Irish Town Songs (ASCAP) and throughout the rest of the world by Blue Mountain Music Ltd. (PRS)
All Rights Reserved

C D5 G C D5

these songs of free - dom? 'Cause all I ev - er have,

3rd time, To Coda

Em C D5 G

re - demp - tion songs.

C D5 G C D5

Re - demp - tion songs. 2. E - man - ci -

C D5 G C D5

Re - demp - tion songs.

Interlude

D.S. al Coda

Em C D5 C D5

3. E - man - ci -

Coda

C D5 Em C D5

All I ev - er have, re - demp - tion

Em C D5 G

songs, these songs of free - dom.

C D5 G C G/B

Songs of free - dom.

Am Am6

Ring of Fire

Words and Music by Merle Kilgore and June Carter

Key of G

Intro

Very fast

Half-time feel

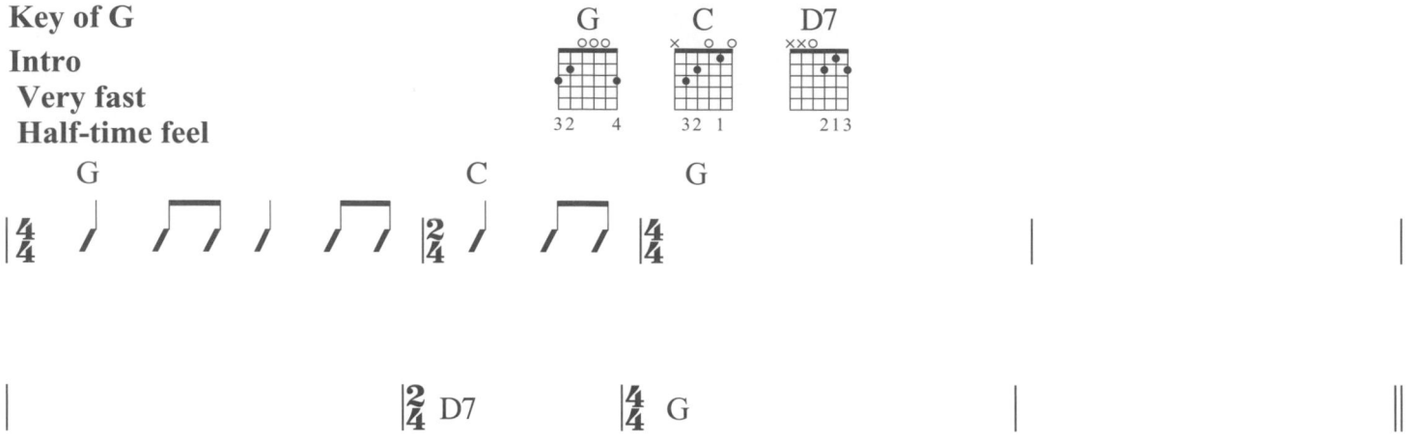

Verse

G C G C G
1. Love is a burn-ing thing and it

D7 G D7 G
makes a fier - y ring.

C G C G
Bound by wild de - sires,

D7 G
I fell in - to a ring of fire.

Chorus

D7 C G
I fell in - to a burn-ing ring of fire. I went

D7 C G
down, down, down, and the flames went high - er. And it

D7 G
burns, burns, burns, the ring of fire,

To Coda

D7 G
the ring of fire.

Copyright © 1962, 1963 Painted Desert Music Corporation, New York
Copyright Renewed
International Copyright Secured All Rights Reserved
Used by Permission

Interlude

|: G | 2/4 C | 4/4 G | |

2nd time, D.S. al Coda

| 2/4 D7 | 4/4 G | :|

Coda **Verse**

G C G C G

2. The taste of love is sweet 2/4 4/4

D7 G D7 G

when hearts like ours meet. 2/4 4/4

C G C G

I fell for you 2/4 like a 4/4 child. 2/4 4/4

D7 G

Oh, but the fire went wild.

Outro-Chorus

D7 C G

|: I fell in - to a burn-ing ring of fire. I went

D7 C G

down, down, down, and the flames went high - er. And it

D7 G

burns, burns, burns, the ring of fire,

D7 G

the ring of fire. :| And it

D7 G D7

burns, burns, burns, the ring of fire, the ring of

Repeat and fade

G D7 G D7

|: fire, the ring of fire, the ring of :|

Run Around

Words and Music by John Popper

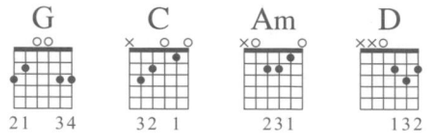

Key of G

Intro

Moderately fast

Verse

G C Am D G
once up - on a mid - night, dear - ie, I woke
shake me and my con - fi - dence 'bout a
- ba, dear, this is the pi - lot speak - ing and I've

C Am D G
with some - thing in my head. I
great a man - y things, but I've been
got some news for you. It seems my

C Am D G
could - n't es - cape the mem - o - ry of a phone
there; I can see it cow - er like a nerv -
ship still stands no mat - ter what you drop, and there ain't a

C Am D G
call and of what you said. Like a
ous ma - gi - cian wait - ing in the wings of a bad
whole lot that you can do. Oh sure, the

C Am D G
game show con - test - ant with a part - ing gift, I could not
play where the he - roes are right and
ban - ner may be torn and the wind's got - ten cold - er.

C Am D G
be - lieve my eyes when I saw
no - bod - y thinks or ex - pects too much.
Per - haps I've grown a lit - tle cyn - i - cal, but, I

C Am D G
through the voice of a trust - ed friend who needs to
Hol - ly - wood's call - ing for the mov - ie rights, sing - ing, "Ba -
know no mat - ter what the wait - ress brings, I shall drink

C Am D G
hu - mor me and tell me lies. Yeah, hu -
- by, let's keep in touch. Hey ba -
it and al - ways be full. Yeah, I will

C Am D G C Am
- mor me and tell me lies. And I'll lie, too, and say I
- by, let's keep in touch." But I want more than a touch; I want
drink it and al - ways be full. Oh, I like cof - fee and I

Copyright © 1994 BLUES TRAVELER PUBLISHING CORP.
All Rights Administered by IRVING MUSIC, INC.
All Rights Reserved Used by Permission

D G C Am D G
don't mind. And | as we seek, so shall | we find. And
you to reach me and | show me all the things no one else | can see, so
like tea. But to be a - ble to en - ter a fi - nal plea. I

C Am D G
when you're feel - ing o - pen I'll still | be here, but
what you feel be - comes mine | as a well. And
still got this dream that you just can't shake. I

C Am D G
not with - out a cer - tain de - gree | of fear of
soon, if we're luck - y, we'd be un - | a - ble to tell what's
love you to the point you can no long - er take. Well, all right,

C Am D G
what will be with | you and me. I still
yours and mine, the | fish - ing's fine, and it does -
o - kay, so be that way. I

C Am D G
can see things, hope | - ful - ly.
n't have to rhyme, so don't you | feed me a line.
hope and pray that there's some - thing left to say. But you,

Chorus

G C Am D G C Am D G
why you wan-na | give me a run a - round? | Is it a sure

To Coda

C Am D G C Am D G
- fire way to speed | things up, when | all it does is slow | me

1. 2.
C Am D G D G
down? | 2. But :

Harmonica Solo 1. - 5. 6. ***D.S. al Coda***

G C Am D G D G
‖: | :‖ 3. Tra - la - la bom -

Coda

C Am D G C Am D G
all it does is slow me | down? Oh, | you. | Why you wan-na

C Am D G C Am D G
give me a run a - round? | Is it a sure | - fire way to speed | things up when

C Am D G C Am D G
all it does is slow | me | down? |

Outro-Harmonica Solo ***Repeat and fade***

‖: G C Am | D G | C Am | D G :‖

Signs

Words and Music by Les Emmerson

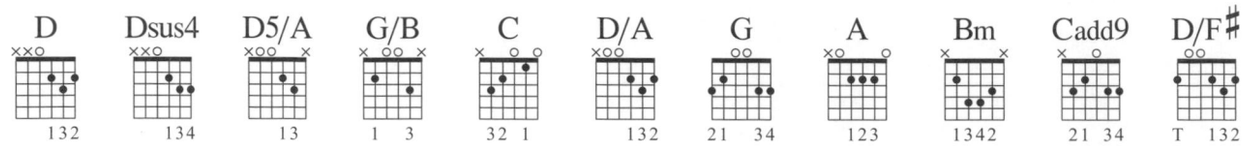

Key of D

Intro

Moderately slow

D Dsus4 D Dsus4 D Dsus4 D D5/A G/B

1. And the
2. And the
3. And the

Verse

C G/B

sign says, "Long - haired, freak - y peo - ple
sign says, "An - y - bod - y caught tres - pass - ing
sign says, "Ev - 'ry - bod - y wel - come, come

D/A G

etc.
need not ap - ply." So I
will be shot on sight." So I
in and kneel down and pray." And then they

D A

tucked my hair up un - der my hat and I
jumped the fence and I yelled at the house, "Hey!
pass a - round the plate at the end of it all, and I

G A

went in to ask him why.
What gives you the right to
did - n't have a pen - ny to pay. A, so I

Bm

He said, "You look like a fine, out - stand - ing young
put up a fence to keep me out or to
got me a pen and a pa - per, and I

G

man, I think you'll do." Uh, so I
keep Moth - er Na - ture in? If
made up my own fuck - in' sign. I said,

D A

took off my hat and said, "I - mag - ine that, huh,
God was here, He'd tell it to your face, 'Man,
"Thank you, Lord, for think - in' a - bout me, I'm a - live

Copyright © 1970 Sony/ATV Music Publishing LLC, Unichappell Music Inc. and Galeneye Music
Copyright Renewed
All Rights on behalf of Sony/ATV Music Publishing LLC Administered by
Sony/ATV Music Publishing LLC, 424 Church Street, Suite 1200, Nashville, TN 37219
All Rights on behalf of Galeneye Music Administered by Unichappell Music Inc.
International Copyright Secured All Rights Reserved

G A
me a work - ing for you." Oh.
you're some kind of sin - ner.'"
and do - in' fine." Oh.

Chorus

D Cadd9 G D G
Signs, signs, ev - 'ry-where a sign fuck - ing up the scen - er - y, break - ing my mind.

3rd time, To Coda

1.

D A Cadd9
Do this, don't do that. Can't you read the sign?

2.

Cadd9 D Dsus4 D/F♯ G G♯ A
6
4fr

Oh. Uh,

Bridge

A G D Dsus4 D
say now, mis - ter, can't you read? You got to have a shirt and tie to get a seat.

w/ Intro pattern

A G D Dsus4 D
You can't watch, no you can't eat. You ain't sup-posed to be here.

Dsus4 D Dsus4 D N.C.
And the sign said, "You got to have a mem - ber - ship

Guitar Solo

D Cadd9 G
card to get in - side." Oo!

D.C. al Coda

D G D A Cadd9

Coda

Cadd9 D Cadd9 G
Signs, signs, ev - 'ry - where a sign fuck -

D G D A
- ing up the scen - er - y, break - ing my mind. Do this, don't do that. Can't you read the sign?

Cadd9 D

Silent Lucidity

Words and Music by Chris DeGarmo

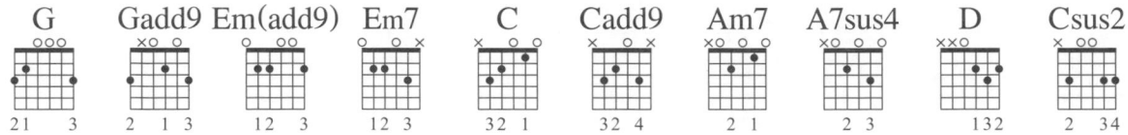

Key of G

Intro

Slow

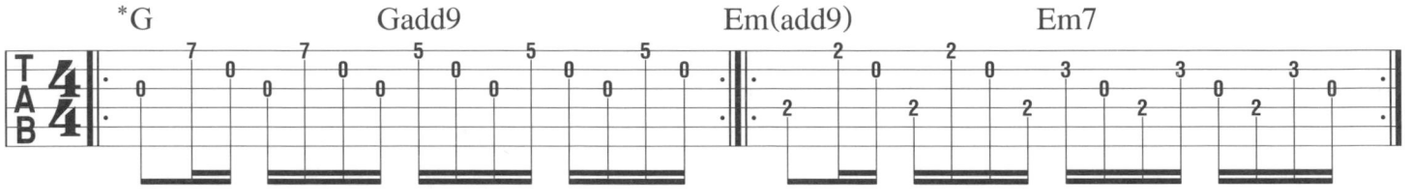

w/ pick & fingers

*Chord symbols reflect implied harmony.

𝄋 Verse

1st time, w/ Intro pattern

2nd & 3rd times, w/ Interlude pattern

G Gadd9 G Gadd9

1. Hush now, don't you cry, wipe a - way the tear-
2. There's a place I like to hide, a door - way that I
3. If you o - pen your mind for me, you won't re - ly on

Em(add9) Em7 Em(add9) Em7

- drop from your eye.
run through in the night.
o - pen eyes to see.

G Gadd9 G Gadd9

You're ly - ing safe in bed, it was all a bad dream
Re - lax child, you were there, but on - ly did - n't
The walls you built with - in, come tum - bling down and a

Em(add9) Em7 Em(add9) Em7

spin - ning in your head.
re - al - ize (it), and you were scared.
new world will be - gin.

C Cadd9 C Cadd9

Your mind tricked you to feel the pain of some - one close to you
It's a place where you will learn to face your fears, re-
Liv - ing twice at once, you learn you're safe from pain in the

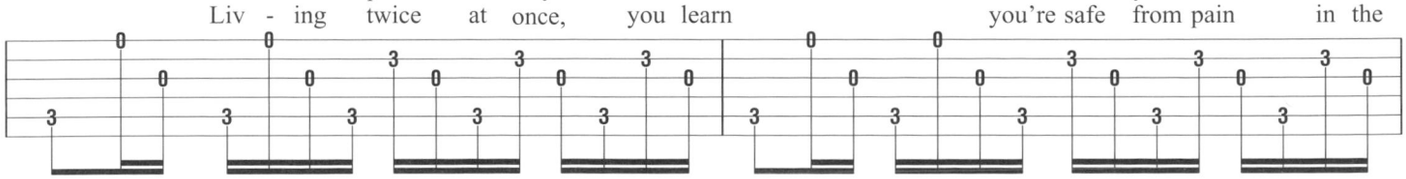

© 1990 SCREEN GEMS-EMI MUSIC INC. and TRI-RYCHE CORP.
All Rights for the U.S. and Canada Controlled and Administered by SCREEN GEMS-EMI MUSIC INC.
All Rights Reserved International Copyright Secured Used by Permission

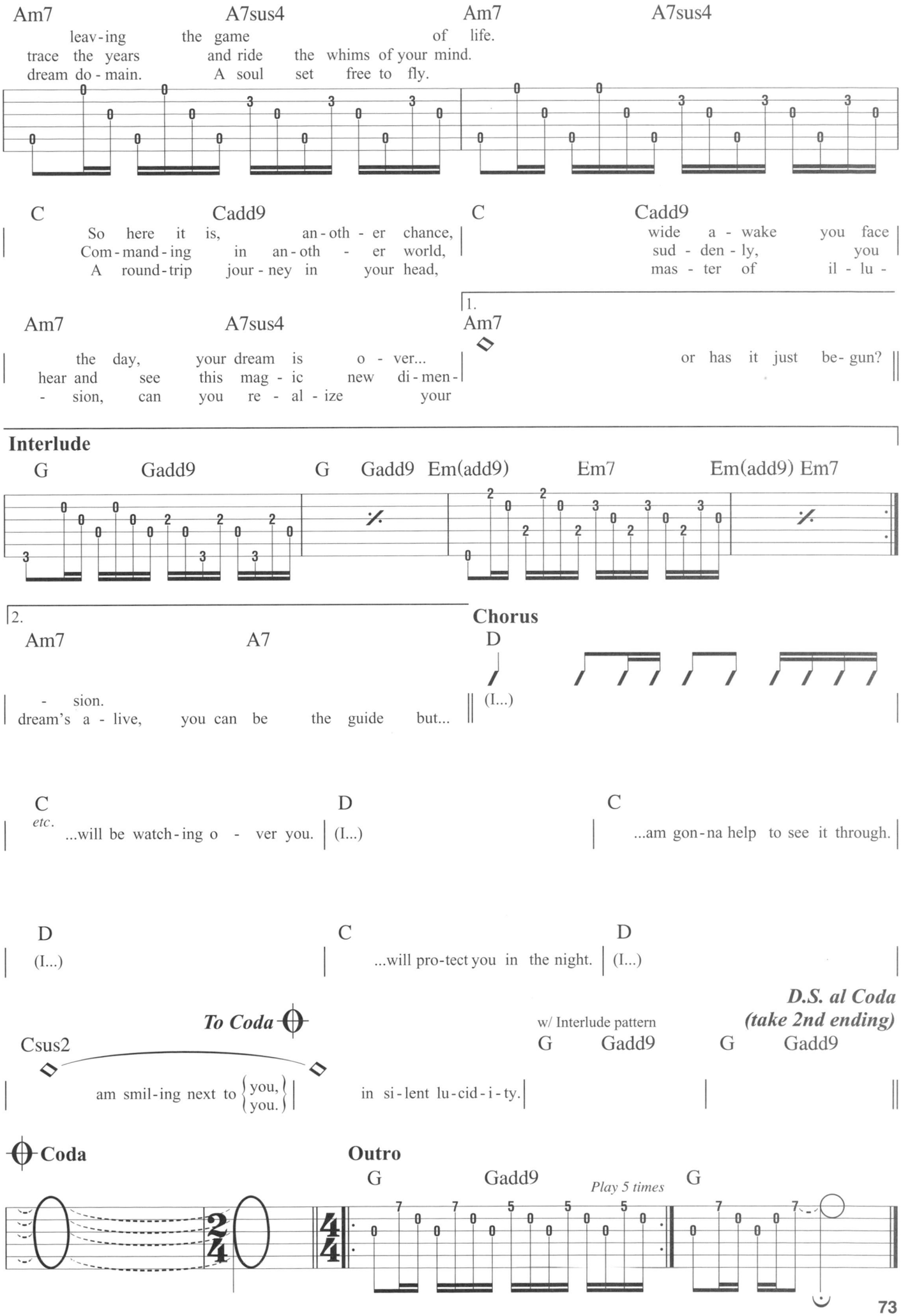
Am7 A7sus4 Am7 A7sus4
leav-ing the game of life.
trace the years and ride the whims of your mind.
dream do-main. A soul set free to fly.
C Cadd9 C Cadd9
So here it is, an-oth-er chance, wide a-wake you face
Com-mand-ing in an-oth-er world, sud-den-ly, you
A round-trip jour-ney in your head, mas-ter of il-lu-
1.
Am7 A7sus4 Am7
the day, your dream is o-ver... or has it just be-gun?
hear and see this mag-ic new di-men-
-sion, can you re-al-ize your
Interlude
G Gadd9 G Gadd9 Em(add9) Em7 Em(add9) Em7
2.
Am7 A7
-sion.
dream's a-live, you can be the guide but...
Chorus
D
(I...)
C D C
etc.
...will be watch-ing o-ver you. (I...) ...am gon-na help to see it through.
D C D
(I...) ...will pro-tect you in the night. (I...)
D.S. al Coda
(take 2nd ending)
To Coda
w/ Interlude pattern
Csus2 G Gadd9 G Gadd9
am smil-ing next to you, you. in si-lent lu-cid-i-ty.
Coda
Outro
G Gadd9 Play 5 times G

Stairway to Heaven

Words and Music by Jimmy Page and Robert Plant

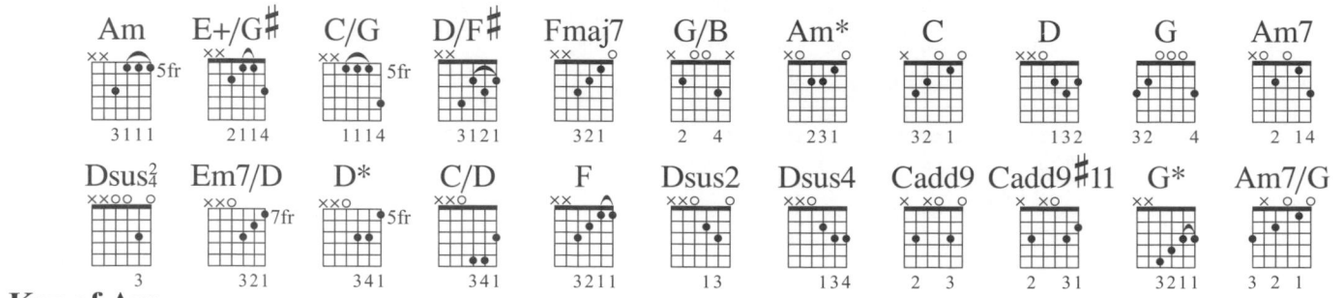

Key of Am

Intro

Slow

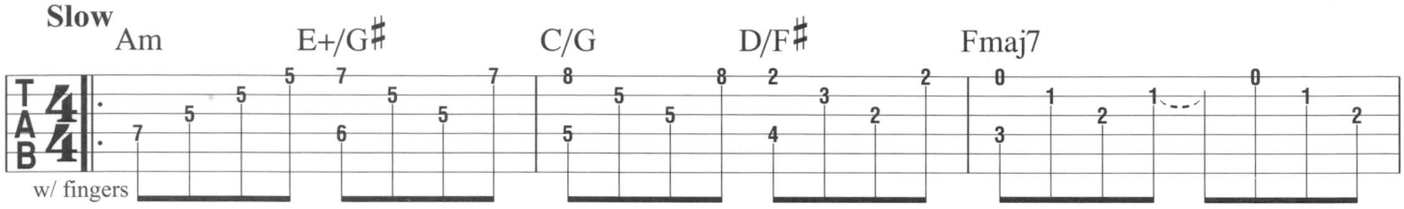

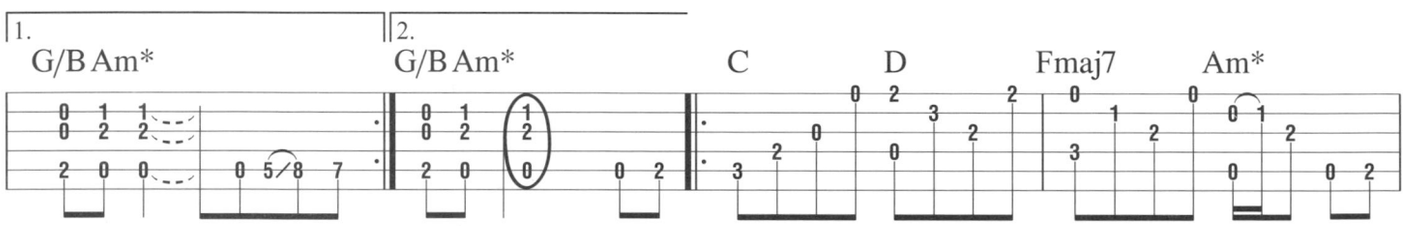

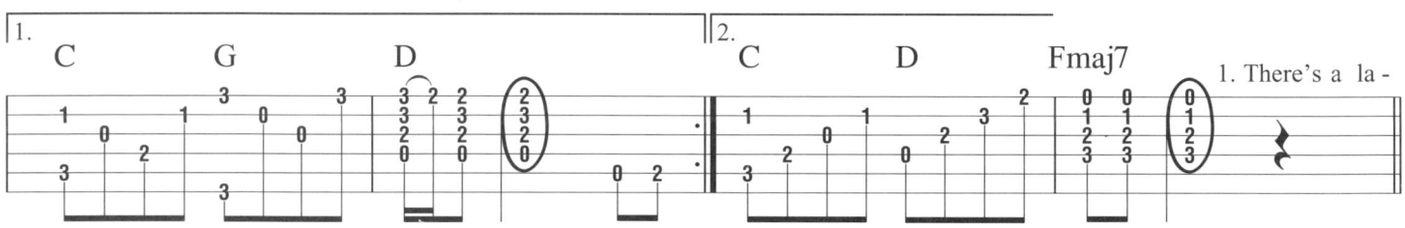

𝄋 Verse w/ Intro pattern

Am E+/G♯ C/G D/F♯ Fmaj7
- dy who's sure all | that glit - ters is gold and she's | buy - ing a stair - way to
tree by the brook, there's a | song - bird who sings, some - times | all of our thoughts are mis -

G/B Am* Am E+/G♯ C/G D/F♯
heav - en. When she | gets there she knows if the | stores are all closed, with a
giv - en. | *Instrumental*

Fmaj7 ***To Coda*** 𝄌 G/B Am* C D Fmaj7 Am*
word she can get what she | came for. | Oo, | oo, and she's
Instrumental ends

C G D C D
buy - ing a stair - way to | heav - en. There's a | sign on the wall, but she

Fmaj7 Am* C D Fmaj7 ***D.S. al Coda***
wants to be sure, 'cause you | know some - times words have two | mean - ings. In a ||

𝄌 Coda

Interlude

Faster w/ Lead Voc. ad lib. on repeats

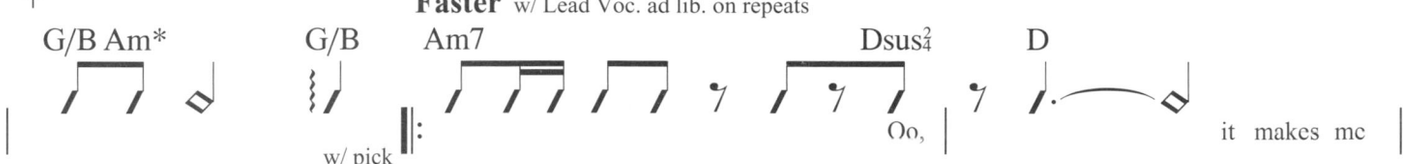

© 1972 (Renewed) FLAMES OF ALBION MUSIC, INC.
All Rights Administered by WB MUSIC CORP.
All Rights Reserved Used by Permission

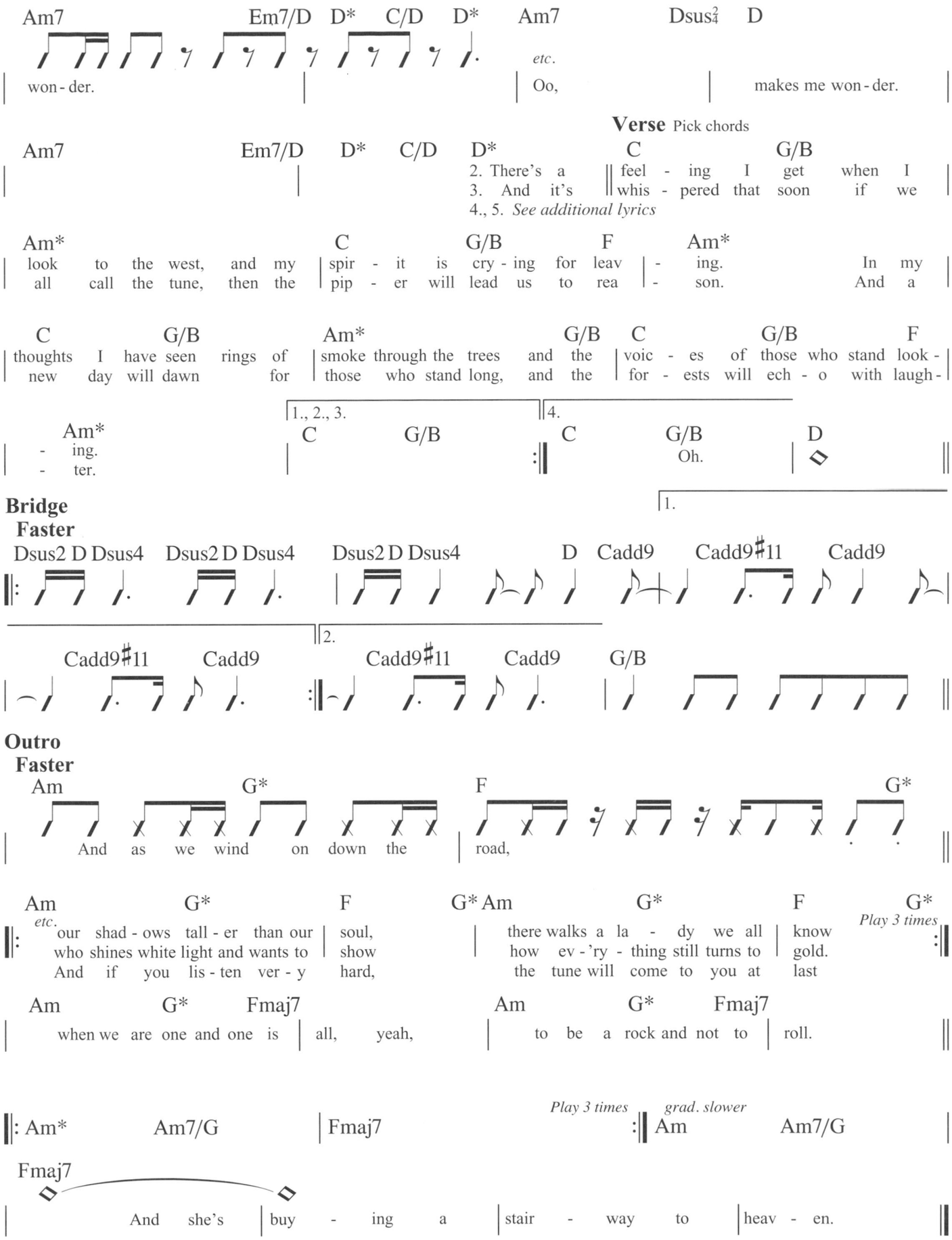

Additional Lyrics

4. If there's a bustle in your hedge-row, don't be alarmed now,
It's just a spring clean for the May queen.
Yes, there are two paths you can go by, but in the long run,
There's still time to change the road you're on.

5. Your head is humming and it won't go, in case you don't know,
The piper's calling you to join him.
Dear lady, can you hear the wind blow, and did you know,
Your stairway lies on the whisp'ring wind.

Take Me Home, Country Roads

Words and Music by John Denver, Bill Danoff and Taffy Nivert

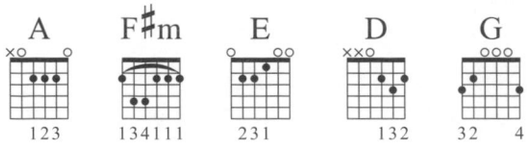

Key of A

Intro

Moderately slow, in 2

Verse

A

1. Al-most
2. All my

let ring throughout

F♯m

heav - en, West Vir-gin - ia,

mem - 'ries gath - er 'round her,

E

Blue Ridge

min - er's

D

Moun - tains, Shen - an - do - ah

la - dy, stran - ger to blue

A

Riv - er.

wa - ter.

etc.

Life is old there,

Dark and dust - y,

F♯m

old - er than the trees,

paint - ed on the sky,

E

young - er than the moun - tains

mist - y taste of moon - shine,

D

grow - in' like a breeze.

tear - drop in my

A

eye.

Coun - try roads,

Chorus

A

take me home

E

to the place

Copyright © 1971; Renewed 1999 BMG Ruby Songs, Anna Kate Deutschendorf, Zachary Deutschendorf,
BMG Rights Management (Ireland) Ltd. and Jesse Belle Denver in the U.S.
All Rights for BMG Ruby Songs, Anna Kate Deutschendorf and Zachary Deutschendorf Administered by BMG Rights Management (US) LLC
All Rights for BMG Rights Management (Ireland) Ltd. Administered by Chrysalis One Music
All Rights for Jesse Belle Denver Administered by WB Music Corp.
International Copyright Secured All Rights Reserved

F♯m D

I be-long: West Vir-gin-

A E

-ia, moun-tain mom-ma. Take me home,

3rd time, To Coda 1

4th time, To Coda 2

D A

coun-try roads. :‖

Bridge

F♯m E A

I hear her voice, in the morn-in' hour she calls me. The

D A E

ra-di-o re-minds me of my home far a-way, and

F♯m G D A

driv-in' down the road I get a feel-in' that I should have been home

E

yes-ter-day, yes-ter-day.

D.S. al Coda 1

Coun-try roads, ‖

Coda 1 *D.S. al Coda 2* **Coda 2**

Coun-try roads, ‖ Take me home, E

A

coun-try roads. Take me home,

E A

coun-try roads.

Tangled Up in Blue

Words and Music by Bob Dylan

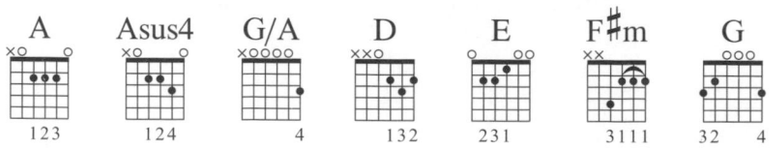

Key of A
Intro
Moderately slow

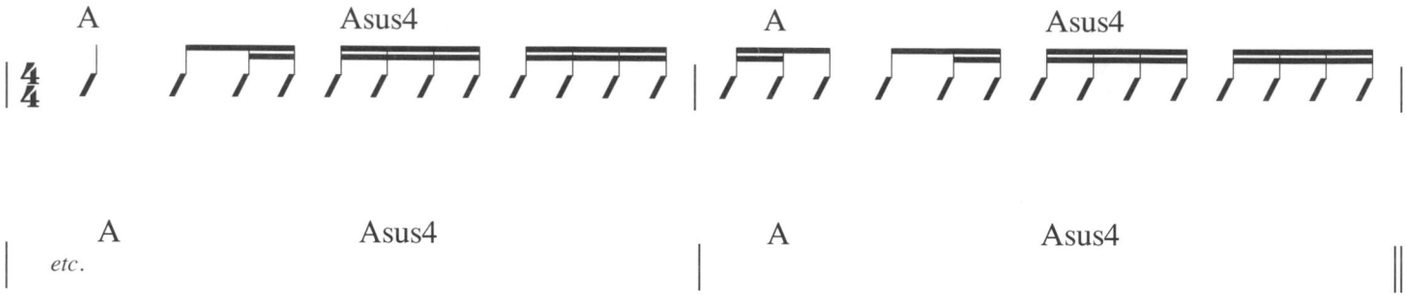

Verse

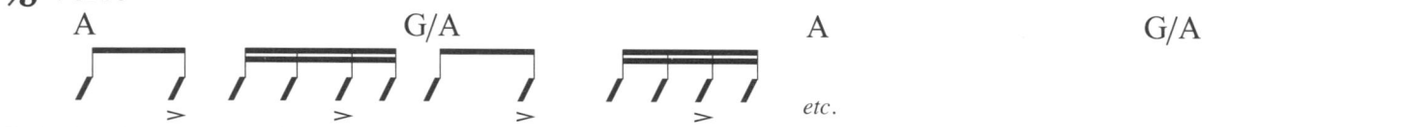

1. Ear - ly one morn - in' the sun was shin - in', I was lay - in' in bed,
2. She was mar - ried when we first met, soon to be di - vorced.
3. - 7. *See additional lyrics*
8. *Instrumental*

A G/A D
won - d'rin' if she'd changed at all, if her hair was still red.
I helped her out of a jam, I guess, but I used a lit - tle too much force. We

A G/A A G/A
Her folks, they said our lives to - geth - er sure was gon - na be rough. They
drove that car as far as we could, a - ban - doned it out West,

A G/A D
nev - er did like Ma - ma's home - made dress, Pa - pa's bank - book was - n't big e - nough. And
split up on a dark sad night, both a - gree - ing it was best.

E F♯m A D
I was stand - in' on the side of the road, rain fall - in' on my shoes.
She turned a - round to look at me as I was walk - in' a - way,

E F♯m A D
Head - ing up for the East Coast, Lord knows I've paid some dues get - tin' through
I heard her say o - ver my shoul - der, "We'll meet a - gain some - day on the av - e - nue,"

8th time, To Coda w/ Intro pattern

E G D A Asus4
tan - gled up in blue.

Copyright © 1974, 1976 Ram's Horn Music
International Copyright Secured All Rights Reserved

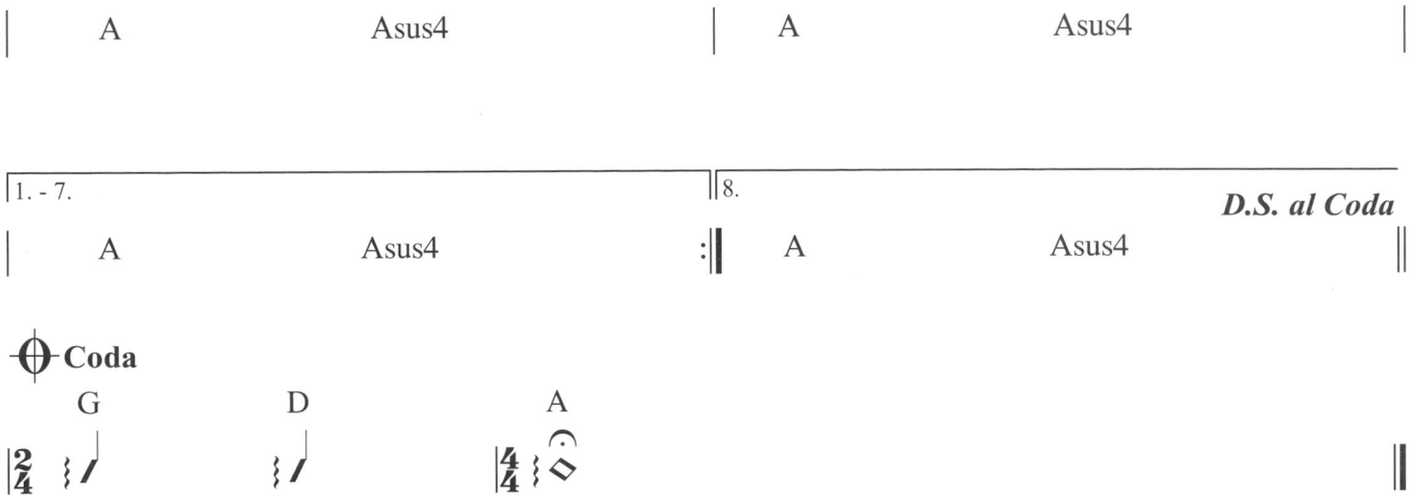

Additional Lyrics

3. I had a job in the great north woods,
Working as a cook for a spell.
But I never did like it all that much
And one day the axe just fell.
So I drifted down to New Orleans
Where I happened to be employed
Workin' for a while on a fishin' boat
Right outside of Delacroix.
But all the while I was alone,
The past was close behind.
I seen a lot of women,
But she never escaped my mind, and I just grew
Tangled up in blue.

4. She was workin' in a topless place
And I stopped in for a beer.
I just kept lookin' at the side of her face
In the spotlight so clear.
And later on when the crowd thinned out,
I's just about to do the same.
She was standin' there in back of my chair,
Said to me, "Don't I know your name?"
I muttered somethin' underneath my breath,
She studied the lines on my face.
I must admit I felt a little uneasy
When she bent down to tie the laces of my shoe
Tangled up in blue.

5. She lit a burner on the stove
And offered me a pipe.
"I thought you'd never say hello," she said,
"You look like the silent type."
Then she opened up a book of poems
And handed it to me,
Written by an Italian poet
From the thirteenth century.
And ev'ry one of them words rang true
And glowed like burnin' coal
Pourin' off of ev'ry page
Like it was written in my soul from me to you
Tangled up in blue.

6. I lived with them on Montague Street
In a basement down the stairs.
There was music in the cafés at night
And revolution in the air.
Then he started into dealing with slaves
And something inside of him died.
She had to sell everything she owned
And froze up inside.
And when finally the bottom fell out
I became withdrawn.
The only thing I knew how to do
Was to keep on keepin' on like a bird that flew
Tangled up in blue.

7. So now I'm goin' back again,
I got to get to her somehow.
All the people we used to know,
They're an illusion to me now.
Some are mathematicians;
Some are carpenter's wives.
Don't know how it all got started,
I don't know what they're doin' with their lives.
But me, I'm still on the road,
Headin' for another joint.
We always did feel the same,
We just saw it from a different point of view
Tangled up in blue.

Tequila Sunrise

Words and Music by Don Henley and Glenn Frey

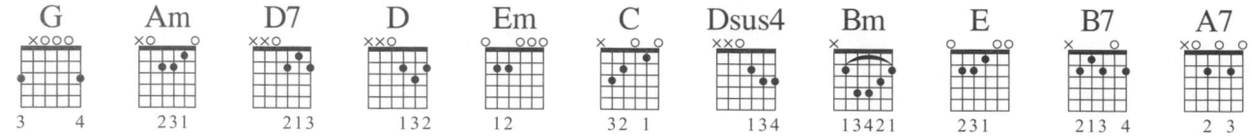

Key of G

Intro

Moderately

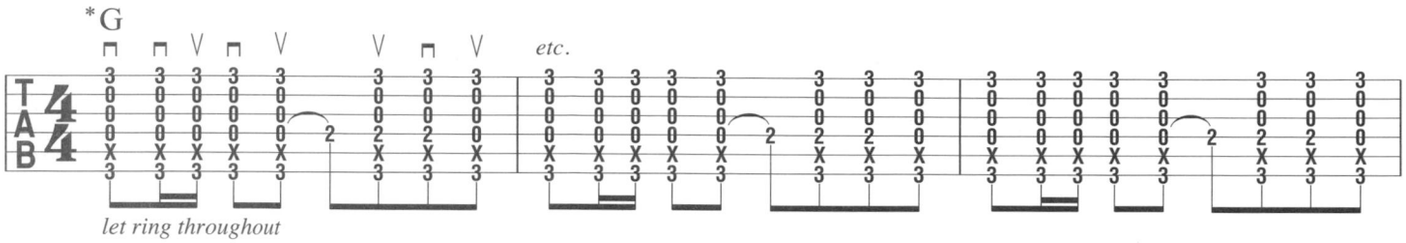

*Chord symbols reflect basic harmony.

| *etc.* | Am | D7 | G | ||

Verse

G D

1. It's an-oth-er te-qui - la sun - rise star-in' slow - ly 'cross the sky,
2. She was-n't just an - oth - er wom - an and I could-n't keep from com - in' on,

Am D G

said good - bye.
it's been so long.

D

He was just a hir - ed hand, work-in' on the dreams he planned to try,
Whoa, and it's a hol - low feel - in' when it comes down to deal - in'

To Coda

Am D7 G

friends, the days go by.
it nev - er ends.

© 1973 (Renewed) CASS COUNTY MUSIC and RED CLOUD MUSIC
All Rights Administered by WARNER-TAMERLANE PUBLISHING CORP.
All Rights Reserved Used by Permission

Chorus

Em C Em C

Ev-'ry night when the sun goes down, just an-oth-er lone-ly boy in town

D.S. al Coda

Em Am D Dsus4

and she's out run-nin' 'round.

Coda

Guitar Solo

G D

Am D G

Bridge

Am D Bm E

Take an-oth-er shot of cour-age. Won-der why the right words nev-er come,

Am B7 Em A7

you just get numb.

Verse

G D

3. And it's an-oth-er te-qui-la sun-rise, this old world still looks the same,

Am D G

an-oth-er frame.

Outro

G

Mm.

Trouble

Words and Music by Ray LaMontagne

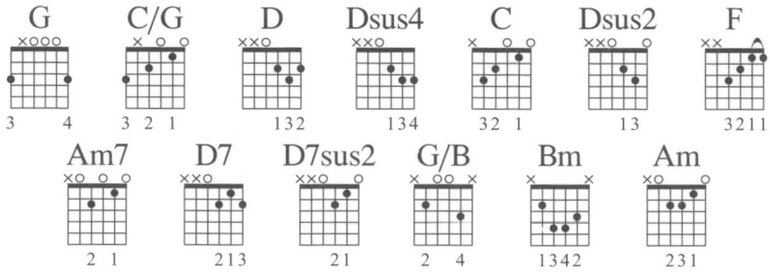

Key of G

Intro

Slow, in 2

G C/G G D Dsus4 D

Play 4 times

Verse

G D G

etc.

1. Trou - ble, | oh, | trou - ble, trou -
2. Trou - ble, | | trou - ble, trou -

C G D

- ble, trou - ble, trou - ble. | Trou - ble been | dog - gin' my soul since the
- ble, trou - ble, trou - ble. | Feels like ev - 'ry | time I get back on my feet, she come a - round

C G D Dsus2 D G

day I was born, ah. | gain. | Wor - ry,
and knock me down a - | | Wor - ry,

D G C G

oh, | wor - ry, | wor - ry, wor - ry, wor - ry. | Wor - ry just
wor - | ry, wor - ry, wor - ry, wor - ry. | Some - times I

D C G D N.C.

will not seem to leave my | mind a - lone. | Well, I've been
swear it feels like this wor - ry | is my on - ly friend. | ||

Chorus

G C F C

a, saved | by | a wom - an. | I've been

G C F C

a, saved | by | a wom - an. | I've been

Copyright © 2004 BMG Monarch and Sweet Mary Music
All Rights Administered by BMG Rights Management (US) LLC
All Rights Reserved Used by Permission

G C *F ** C
a, saved by a wom - an. She won't

*2nd time, substitute C.
**2nd time, substitute G/B.

Am7 D7 D7sus4 D7 D7sus2
let me go, she won't let me go, now. She won't

Am7 D7
let me go, she won't let me go now,

1. D7sus2 now. 2. now.

Intro (2 times)

4

Bridge

1. 2.
C Bm Am G Am
Oh. Ah. Mm, she

G C/G G C/G G C/G
good to me, now. She gave me love and af-

1. 2.
G C/G G C/G G C/G
fec - tion. Say she fec - tion. I said, I love her. Yes, I

G C/G G C/G G C/G
love her. I said, I love her. I said, I love. She

G C/G G C/G G C/G
good to me, now. She good to me. She

Outro

G C/G G C/G G C/G G C/G
good to me. Mm, mm, mm,

G C/G G C/G G
mm.

grad. slower

Truckin'

Words and Music by Jerry Garcia, Robert Hunter, Phil Lesh and Bob Weir

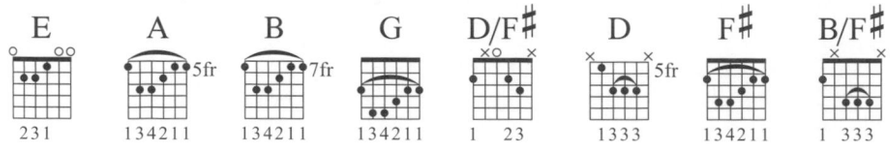

Key of E

Intro

Moderately (♩♫ = ♩³♪)

N.C.(E)

E

Play 4 times

Riff **End Riff**

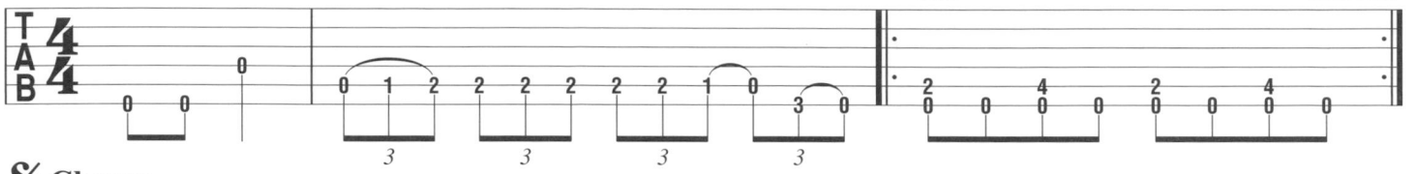

𝄋 Chorus

w/ riff — E — strum chords — A

|: 1. Truck - in', got my | chips cashed in, keep | truck - in', like the |
2. Dal - las got a | soft ma - chine, | Hous - ton, too close to |

4., 5. *See additional lyrics*

B

| doo - dah man. To - | geth - er, more or | less in line. |
New Or - leans. | New York got the | ways an' means, and |

A — w/ riff — E

| Just keep truck - in' on. | | | | | | ||
just won't let you be. | | | | | | |

Verse

E

| 1. Ar - rows of ne - on and flash - ing mar quees out on | Main Street. Chi - |
2. Most of the cats that you meet on the street speak of | true love. |

4., 5. *See additional lyrics*

| ca - go, New - York, De - troit and it's all on the | same street. Your |
Most of the time, they're sit - ting and cry - ing at | home. |

| typ - i - cal cit - y in - volved in a typ - i - cal | day - dream. |
One of these days they know they've got - ta get | go - in' |

| Hang it up and see what to - mor - row brings. | :||
out of the door and down to the street all a - | lone. |

Bridge

strum chords

A G D/F♯ A

| Some - times the lights all | 𝄾 shin - in' on | 𝄿 me. | | |

Copyright © 1971 ICE NINE PUBLISHING CO., INC.
Copyright Renewed
All Rights Administered by UNIVERSAL MUSIC CORP.
All Rights Reserved Used by Permission

D A G D/F♯ A

Oth - er times I can bare - ly see.

D B F♯ B/F♯ F♯

Late - ly it oc - curs to me, what a

w/ riff

A E

long, strange trip it's been.

Chorus

strum chords

E A

3. Truck - in' like the doo - dah man, once told me you got to
6. Truck - in', I'm a go - in' home. Whoa, whoa, ba - by, back where

B

play your hand. Some - times the cards ain't worth a dime,
I be - long. Back home, sit down and patch my bones and

w/ riff

A E

if you don't lay 'em down.
get back truck - in' on.

To Coda

Verse

E

3. What in the world ev-er be-came of sweet Jane? She lost her spar-kle, you know she is-n't the

same. Liv-in' on Reds, Vit-a-min C and co - caine,

D.S. al Coda
(take repeat)

all a friend can say is ain't it a shame.

Coda

Outro-Guitar Solo

Repeat and fade

E

Additional Lyrics

Chorus 4 Truckin' up to Buffalo,
Been thinkin' you got to mellow slow.
Takes time to pick a place to go,
And just keep truckin' on.

4. Sittin' and starin' out of the hotel window,
Got a tip they're gonna kick the door in again.
I'd like to get some sleep before I travel,
But if you got a warrant I guess you're gonna come in.

Chorus 5 Busted down on Bourbon Street,
Set up like a bowlin' pin.
Knocked down, it gets to wearing thin,
They just won't let you be.

5. You're sick of hangin' around an' you'd like to travel.
Get tired of travelin', you want to settle down.
I guess they can't revoke your soul for tryin'.
Get out of the door, light out and look all around.

Wagon Wheel

Words and Music by Bob Dylan and Ketch Secor

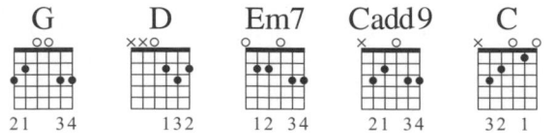

Capo II

Key of A (Capo Key of G)

Intro

Moderately fast (♩♩ = ♩♪)

G D Em7 Cadd9

etc.

G D Cadd9

2. I'm

Verse

3rd time, let chords ring

G D Em7

1. Head-in' down south to the land of the pines, I'm thumb-in' my way in-to North
run-nin' from the cold up in New Eng-land. I was born to be a fid-dler in an old
3. Walk-in' to the south out-ta Ro-a-noke, I caught a truck-er out-ta Phil-ly, had a

C G D

Car-o-li-na, star-in' up the road and pray to God I see head-
time string band. My ba-by plays the gui-tar, I pick a ban-jo now.
nice long toke. But he's, a, head-in' west from the Cum-ber-land Gap to

C G

-lights. I made it down the coast in
Oh, north coun-try win-ters keep, a,
John-son Cit-y, Ten-nes-see. I got-ta get a move on be-

D Em7 C

sev-en-teen hours, pick-in' me a bou-quet of dog-wood flow-ers, and I'm, a,
get-tin' me down, lost my mon-ey play-in' pok-er so I had to leave town. But I ain't,
-fore the sun. I hear my ba-by call-in' my name and I know that she's the on-ly one. And

3rd time, To Coda 1

G D C

hop-in' for Ral-eigh, I can see my ba-by to-night. more. So, rock
a, turn-in' back to liv-in' that old life no
if I die in Ra-leigh, at least I will die free.

Copyright © 2004 Special Rider Music and Blood Donor Music
International Copyright Secured All Rights Reserved

𝄋 Chorus

G D Em7 C

me, ma-ma, like a wag-on wheel. Rock me, ma-ma, an-y way you feel. Hey,

G D C

ma-ma, rock me. Rock

G D Em7 C

me, ma-ma, like the wind and the rain. Rock me, ma-ma, like a south-bound train. Hey,

3rd time, To Coda 2 1. 2.

G D C

ma-ma, rock me. :‖

Solos

‖: G D Em7 C

1. 2.

D.S. al Coda 1

G D C :‖

Coda 1

Chorus

Half-time feel

G D Em7 C

me, ma-ma, like a wag-on wheel. Rock me, ma-ma, an-y way you feel.
me, ma-ma, like the wind and the rain. Rock me, ma-ma, like a south-bound train. Hey,

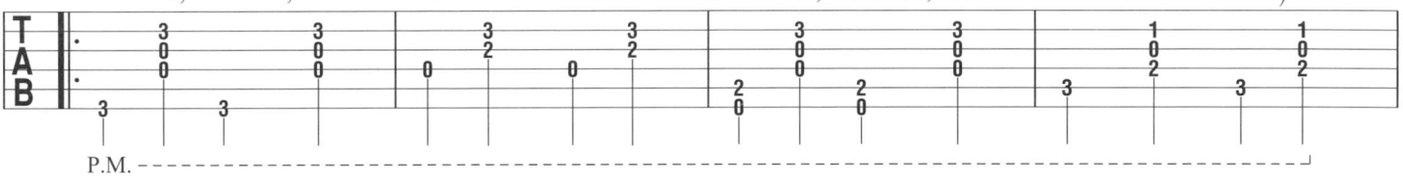

1. 2.

D.S.S. al Coda 2

2nd time, w/ Intro pattern

End half-time feel

G D C

etc.

ma-ma, rock me. Oh, rock :‖ Oh, rock ‖

Coda 2

Outro

‖: G D Em7 Cadd9

Repeat and fade

G D Cadd9 :‖

Wake Up Little Susie

Words and Music by Boudleaux Bryant and Felice Bryant

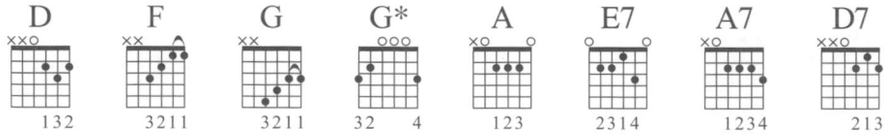

Tune down 1/2 step:
(low to high) E♭-A♭-D♭-G♭-B♭-E♭

Key of D

Intro

Fast (♩♫ = ♩³♪)

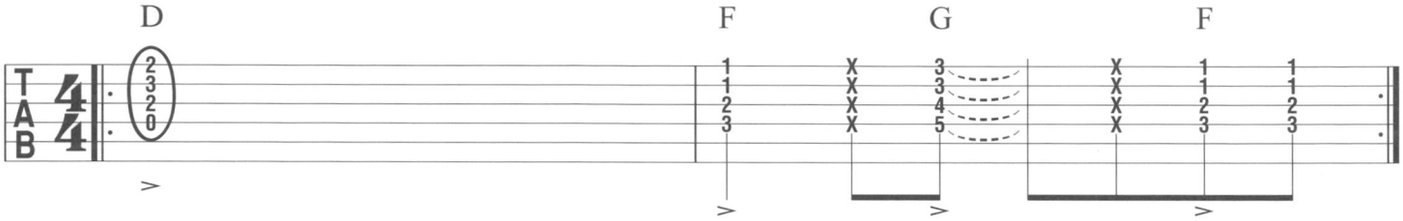

Chorus

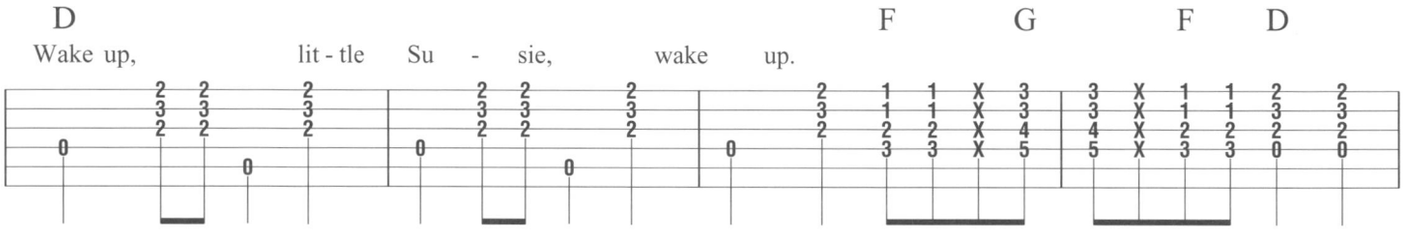

Wake up, lit - tle Su - sie, wake up.

etc.

Wake up, lit - tle | Su - sie, wake | up. | 1. We've / 2. The

G* D G* D G*

both been sound a - | sleep; wake up, | lit - tle Su - sie, and | weep. The mov -
mov - ie was - n't so | hot, it did | - n't have much of a | plot. We fell

D G* D G* D G*

- ie's o - ver, it's | four o' - clock and | we're in trou-ble deep. | shot. } Wake up, lit - tle
a - sleep, our | goose is cooked, our | rep - u - ta - tion is

A G* A

Su - sie. | Wake up, lit - tle | Su - sie. | Well, ||

Copyright © 1957 by HOUSE OF BRYANT PUBLICATIONS, Gatlinburg, TN
Copyright Renewed
All Foreign Rights Controlled by SONY/ATV MUSIC PUBLISHING LLC
All Rights on behalf of SONY/ATV MUSIC PUBLISHING LLC
Administered by SONY/ATV MUSIC PUBLISHING LLC, 424 Church Street, Suite 1200, Nashville, TN 37219
International Copyright Secured All Rights Reserved

Verse

A E7 A E7 A

what are we gon-na tell your ma - ma? What are we gon-na tell your pa?

E7 A N.C.

What are we gon-na tell our friends when they say, "Ooh, la, la?" Wake up, lit - tle

To Coda

D A7 D A7

Su - sie. Wake up, lit - tle Su - sie. Well, I

Bridge

D D7

told your ma - ma that you'd be in by ten. Well,

G*

Su - sie, ba - by, looks like we goofed a - gain. Wake up, lit - tle

A7 G* A7 N.C.

Su - sie. Wake up, lit - tle Su - sie. We got - ta go

D.S. al Coda

D F G F D F G F

home.

Coda

A7 D

Wake up, lit - tle Su - sie.

Outro

D F G D F G

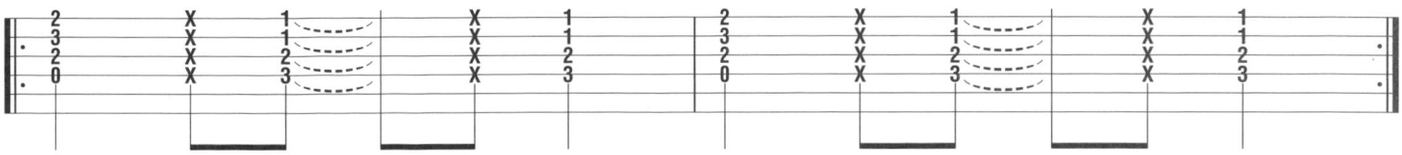

Repeat and fade

D F G F D F G F

We Can Work It Out

Words and Music by John Lennon and Paul McCartney

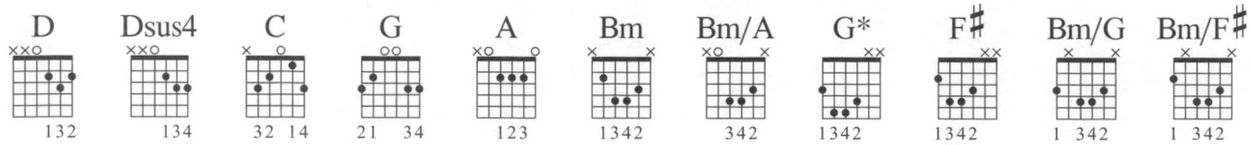

Key of D

Verse

Moderately

D Dsus4 D Dsus4

1. Try to see it my way. Do I have to keep on talk - ing
2. Think of what you're say - ing. You can get it wrong and still you think

etc.

C D Dsus4 D

'til I can't go on? While you see it your way,
that it's al - right. Think of what I'm say - ing.

Dsus4 C D

run a risk of know-ing that our love may soon be gone.
We can work it out and get it straight or say good - night.

G D G A

We can work it out. We can work it out.

Bridge

Bm Bm/A G*

etc.

Life is ver - y short and there's no time

F♯ Bm Bm/A Bm/G Bm/F♯

for fuss - ing and fight - ing, my friend.

Copyright © 1965 Sony/ATV Music Publishing LLC
Copyright Renewed
All Rights Administered by Sony/ATV Music Publishing LLC, 424 Church Street, Suite 1200, Nashville, TN 37219
International Copyright Secured All Rights Reserved

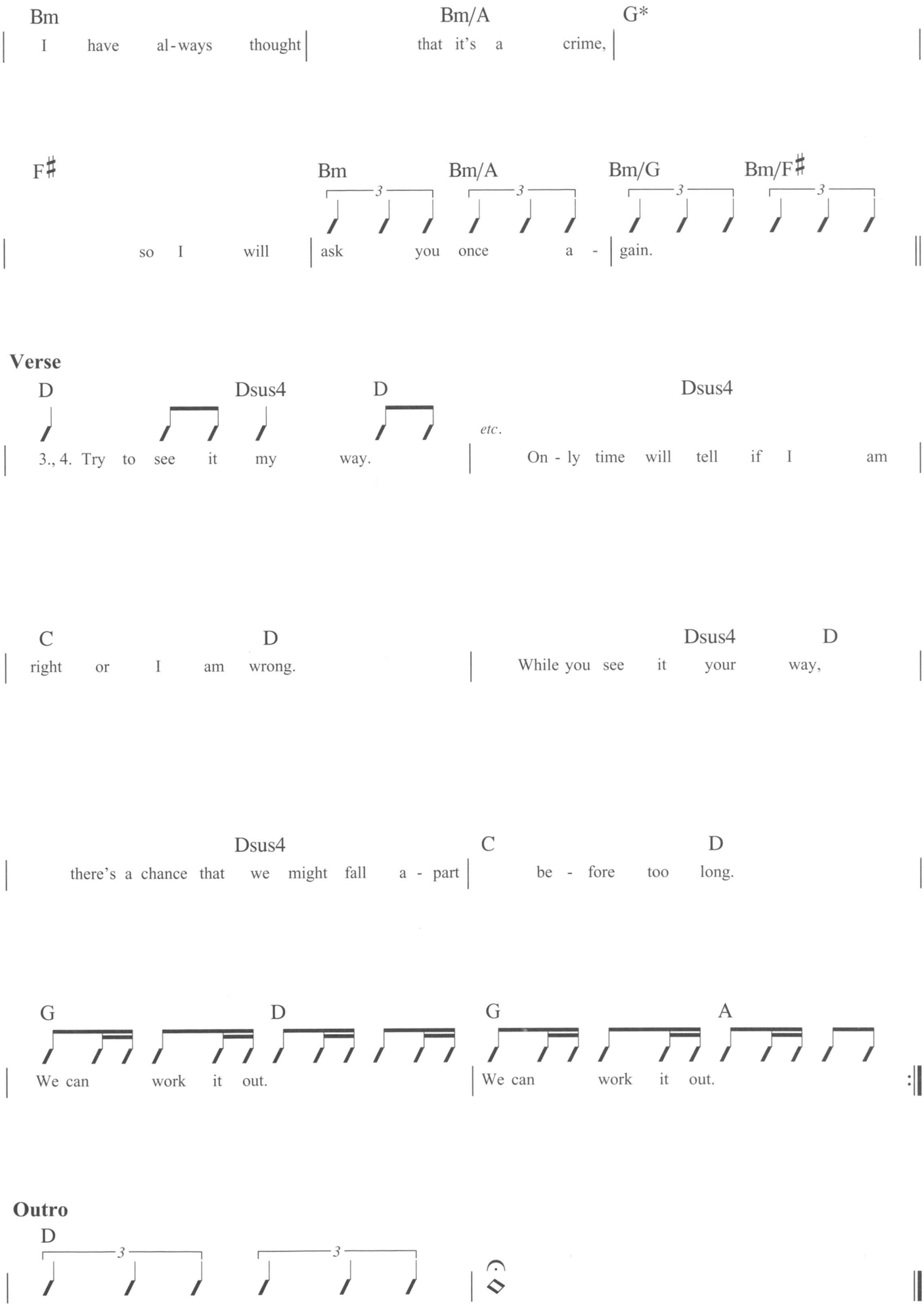
Bm
Bm/A
G*
I have al-ways thought
that it's a crime,
F♯
Bm
Bm/A
Bm/G
Bm/F♯
so I will
ask you once a -
gain.
Verse
D
Dsus4
D
Dsus4
etc.
3., 4. Try to see it my way.
On - ly time will tell if I am
C
D
right or I am wrong.
Dsus4
D
While you see it your way,
Dsus4
C
D
there's a chance that we might fall a - part
be - fore too long.
G
D
G
A
We can work it out.
We can work it out.
Outro
D

What I Got

Words and Music by Brad Nowell, Eric Wilson, Floyd Gaugh and Lindon Roberts

Key of D

Intro

Moderately slow (♩♩ = ♪♪)

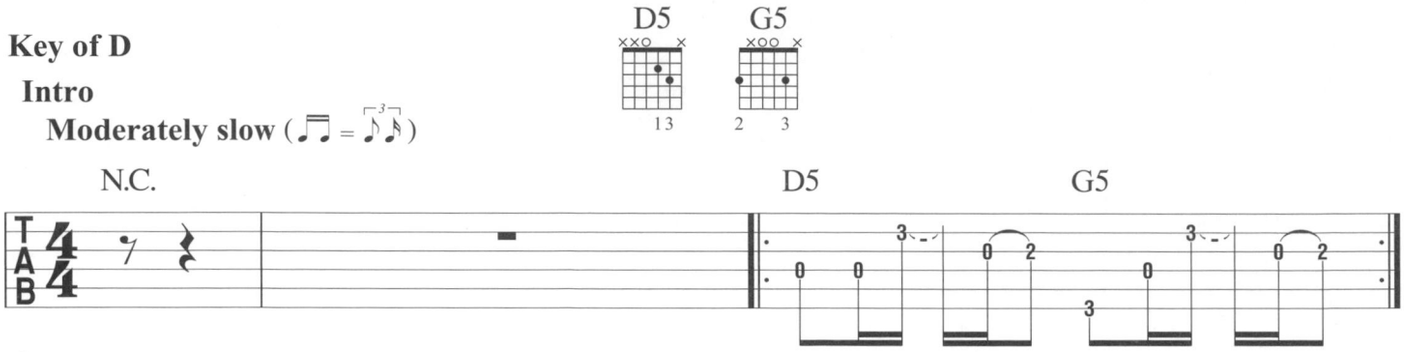

Verse

D5 G5 D5 G5

1. Ear - ly in the morn - in', ris - in' to the street.
is (too short) so love the one you got, 'cause you might get run o - ver or you might get shot.
3. Why, I don't cry when my dog runs a-way. I don't get an-gry at the bills I have to pay.

D5 G5 D5 G5

etc.

Light me up that cig - a - rette and I strap shoes on my feet.
Nev-er start no stat-ic, I just get it off my (chest.) Nev-er had to bat-tle with no bul-let-proof (vest.)
I don't get an-gry when my mom smokes pot, hits the bot-tle and goes right to the rock.

D5 G5 D5 G5

Got to find a rea - son, rea - son things went wrong.
Take a small ex - am - ple, take a ti - ti - ti-tip from me, take all of your mon - ey, give it all (to char-i - ty...) Love
Fuck-in' and fight-in', it's all the same. Liv - in' with Lou-ie Dog's the on-ly way to stay sane.

3rd time, To Coda ⊕

D5 G5 D5 G5

Got to find a rea - son why my mon-ey's all gone.
is what I got, it's with - in my reach, and the Sub - lime style's still straight from Long Beach. It all comes
Let the lov-in', let the lov - in' come back

D5 G5 D5 G5

I got a Dal - ma - tion, and I can still get high.
back to you, you fin-'ly get what you de-serve. Try and test that, you're bound to get served.

D5 G5 D5 G5

I can play the gui - tar like a moth - er - fuck - in' ri - ot.
Love's what I got, don't start a ri - ot. You feel it when the dance gets hot.

Copyright © 1996 SONGS OF UNIVERSAL, INC., GASOLINE ALLEY MUSIC, LOU DOG PUBLISHING, FLOYD I. GAUGH III PUBLISHING, ERIC WILSON PUBLISHING, UNIVERSAL MUSIC - CAREERS and HALFPINT MUSIC
All Rights for GASOLINE ALLEY MUSIC, LOU DOG PUBLISHING, FLOYD I. GAUGH III PUBLISHING and ERIC WILSON PUBLISHING Controlled and Administered by SONGS OF UNIVERSAL, INC.
All Rights for HALFPINT MUSIC in the U.S. Controlled and Administered by UNIVERSAL MUSIC - CAREERS
All Rights Reserved Used by Permission

1.

Interlude

D5 G5 | D5 G5 | D5 G5

2.

Chorus

D5 G5 | D5 G5 | D5 G5

2. Well, life :‖ Lov - in' is what I got. | I said re-mem-ber that.

D5 G5 | D5 G5 | D5 G5

Lov - in' is what I got. | and re-mem-ber that. | Lov - in' is what I got.

D.S. al Coda

D5 G5 | D5 G5 | D5 G5

I said re-mem-ber that. | Lov - in' is what I got, | I got, I got, I got. ‖

Coda

*D5 | D5 G5 | D5 G5

to me. ‖

*Let chord ring.

D5 G5 | D5 G5 | **D5

'Cause ‖

**Let chord ring.

Chorus

D5 G5 | D5 G5 | D5 G5

lov - in' is what I got. | I said re-mem-ber that. | Lov - in' is what I got.

D5 G5 | D5 G5 | D5 G5

and re-mem-ber that. | Lov - in' is what I got. | I said re-mem-ber that.

Outro ***Repeat and fade***

D5 G5 | D5 G5 | D5 G5 | D5 G5

Lov - in' is what I got, | I got, I got, I got. ‖: | :‖

Wild World

Words and Music by Cat Stevens

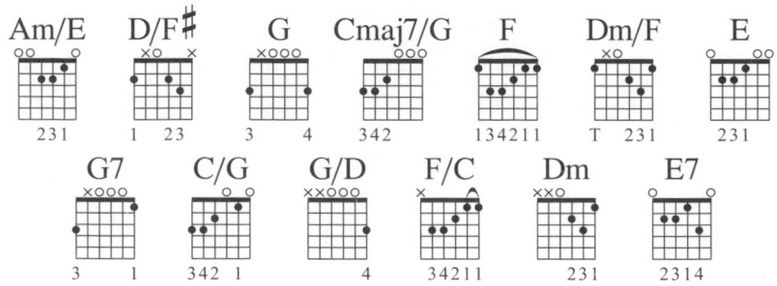

Key of C
Intro
Moderately slow

Am/E D/F♯ G Cmaj7/G

P.M. - - - - P.M. - - - - *etc.*

4/4 La, la, la, la, la, la, la, la, la, la. | La, la, la, la, la, la, la, la, la, la.

F Dm/F E

La, la, la, la, la, la, la, la, la, la, | la. ||

𝄋 Verse

Am/E D/F♯ G Cmaj7/G

|: 1. Now that I've lost ev - 'ry - thing to you, you say you want to start some - thing
2. You know I've seen a lot of what the world can do and it's break - in' my heart in
3. *Instrumental (w/ Voc. ad lib.)*

F Dm/F E

new, and it's break - in' my heart you're leav - in'. Ba - by, I'm griev - in'.
two be - cause I nev - er want to see you sad, girl. Don't be a bad girl.
Instrumental ends Ba - by, I love you.

Am/E D/F♯ G Cmaj7/G

But if you want to leave, take good care. Hope you have a lot of nice things to wear,
But if you want to leave, take good care. Hope you make a lot of nice friends out

F Dm/F E G

but then a lot of nice things turn 3/4 bad out there.
there, but just re - mem - ber there's a lot of bad, and be - ware.

Chorus

N.C.(G7) C/G G/D F/C N.C.

Oo, ba - by, ba - by, it's a wild world.

Copyright © 1970 Cat Music Ltd. and BMG Rights Management (UK) Ltd., a BMG Chrysalis company
Copyright Renewed
All Rights Reserved Used by Permission

G F C/G N.C.

It's hard to get by just up - on a smile.

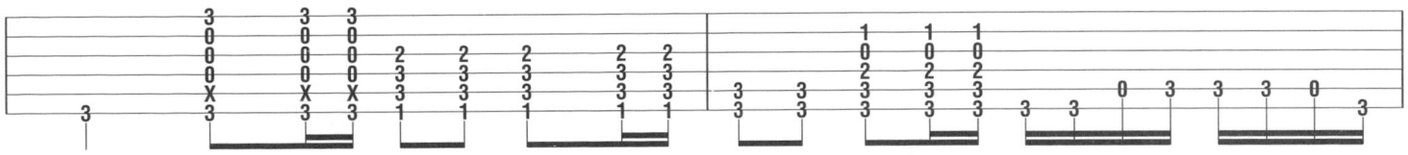

3rd time, To Coda ⊕

C/G G/D F/C N.C.

Oo, ba - by, ba - by, it's a wild world.

1.

G F/C C/G Dm E7

I'll al - ways re - mem - ber you like a child, girl. :‖

2.

D.S. al Coda

N.C. G F C/G Dm E7

And I'll al - ways re - mem - ber you like a child, girl. ‖

⊕ **Coda**

N.C. G F C/G Dm E7

And I'll al - ways re - mem - ber you like a child, girl.

C/G G/D F/C N.C.

Oo, ba - by, ba - by, it's a wild world.

G F C/G N.C.

It's hard to get by just up - on a smile.

C/G G/D F/C N.C.

Oo, ba - by, ba - by, it's a wild world.

N.C. G F C/G

And I'll al - ways re - mem - ber you like a child, girl. ‖

Wish You Were Here

Words and Music by Roger Waters and David Gilmour

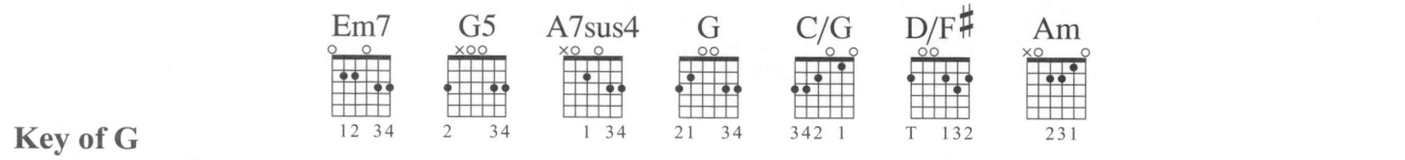

Key of G
Intro
Slow

Em7 G5

2nd & 3rd times, Instrumental solo

Em7 A7sus4 Em7

A7sus4 G

1.

2.

Verse

C/G D/F♯

1. So, so you think you can tell heav - en from hell,
3. How I wish, how I wish you were here. We're just

Am G

two lost souls swim-ming in a fish - bowl, blue skies from pain. Can you tell a green
year af - ter year.

D/F♯ C/G

field Run-ning o - ver the same old ground, from a cold steel rail, a smile from a veil?
what have we found? The same old

© 1975 (Renewed) ROGER WATERS OVERSEAS LTD. and PINK FLOYD MUSIC PUBLISHERS, INC.
All Rights for ROGER WATERS OVERSEAS LTD. in the U.S. and Canada Administered by WARNER-TAMERLANE PUBLISHING CORP.
All Rights Reserved Used by Permission

To Coda ⊕

Am | G

fears, Do you think you can tell? wish you were here. | 2. Did they get you to trade ||

Verse

C/G | D/F♯

your he - roes for | ghosts, hot ash - es for trees, |

Am | G

hot air for a cool | breeze, cold com-fort for change? |

D/F♯ | C/G

Did you ex - change | a walk-on part in the war |

D.S. al Coda
(take 2nd ending)

Am | G

for a lead role in a cage? | ||

Outro-Guitar Solo

w/ Intro pattern

||: Em7 | G5 | Em7 | G5 |

| Em7 | A7sus4 | Em7 |

Repeat and fade

| A7sus4 | G | | :||

Yellow

Words and Music by Guy Berryman, Jon Buckland, Will Champion and Chris Martin

Tuning:
(low to high) E-A-B-G-B-D♯

B Badd4 F♯6add11 Emaj13 Emaj7 G♯m F♯m11

Key of B

Intro

Moderately slow

*B Badd4

*Chord symbols reflect combined harmony.

B Badd4 F♯6add11

etc.

Emaj13 Emaj7 B Badd4

Verse

B F♯6add11

1. Look at the stars; look how they shine for you

Emaj7

and ev - 'ry - thing you do. Yeah, they were all yel - low.

B F♯6add11

I came a - long; I wrote a song for you
2. I swam a - cross, I jumped a - cross for you.

Emaj7

and all the things you do, and it was called "Yel - low."
Oh, what a thing to do, 'cause you were all yel - low.

B F♯6add11

I drew a line, So then I took my turn.
I drew a line for you.

Emaj7

Oh, what a thing to have done, and it was all yel - low.
Oh, what a thing to do. And it was all yel - low.

Copyright © 2000 by Universal Music Publishing MGB Ltd.
All Rights in the United States and Canada Administered by Universal Music - MGB Songs
International Copyright Secured All Rights Reserved

| B | Badd4 B ||

Chorus

Emaj7 | Your skin,
G♯m F♯6add11 | oh yeah, your skin and bones
Emaj7 | turn in -

G♯m F♯6add11 | - to some - thing beau - ti - ful.
Emaj7 | Do you know,
G♯m F♯6add11 | you know I love you so? / for you I bleed my - self

Interlude

Emaj7 | dry,
You know I love you so. / for you I bleed my - self
B || dry.

| Badd4 | F♯6add11 | Emaj13 |

1. 2.

Emaj7 | B | Badd4 :|| Badd4 It's ||

Outro

||: B { true. }
Badd4 | Look how they shine for
F♯6add11 | you,

look how they shine for
Emaj13 | you,
1. Emaj7 | look how they shine for... :||

2. Emaj7 | look how they shine.
B | Look at the stars;
look how they shine for

F♯m11 | you,
and all the things that you
Emaj7 | do. ||

Yesterday

Words and Music by John Lennon and Paul McCartney

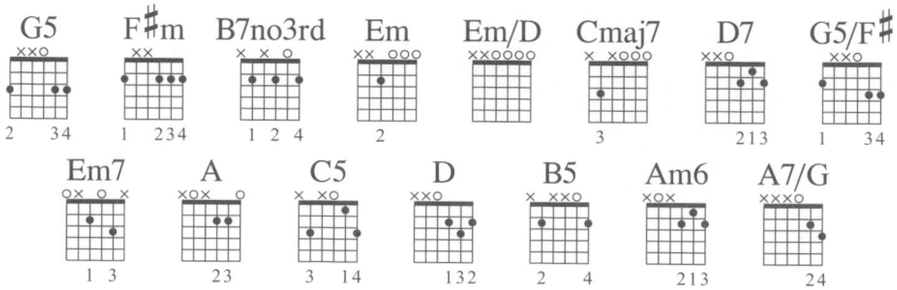

Tune down 1 step:
(low to high) D-G-C-F-A-D

Key of G

Intro

Moderately

G5

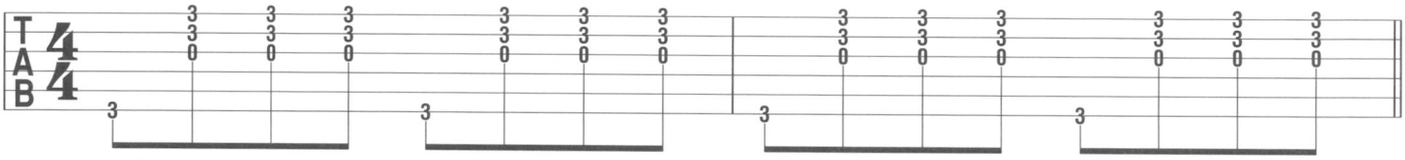

w/ fingers
let ring throughout

Verse

G5 *etc.* | F♯m B7(no3rd) | Em | Em/D

1. Yes - ter - day, all my trou - bles seemed so far a - way,
2. Sud - den - ly, I'm not half the man I used to be

Cmaj7 D7 | G5 | G5/F♯ Em7 | A

now it looks as though they're here to stay. Oh, I be - lieve in
There's a shad - ow hang - ing o - ver me. Oh, yes - ter - day came

Bridge

C5 G5 | F♯m B7(no3rd) | Em D C5 B5

yes - ter - day. Why she had to go, I don't
sud - den - ly.

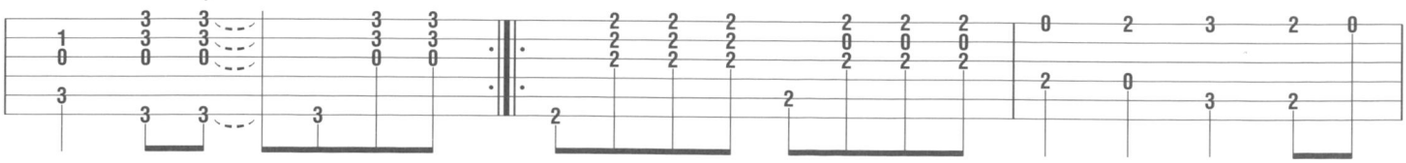

Copyright © 1965 Sony/ATV Music Publishing LLC
Copyright Renewed
All Rights Administered by Sony/ATV Music Publishing LLC, 424 Church Street, Suite 1200, Nashville, TN 37219
International Copyright Secured All Rights Reserved

Am6 D7 G5 F♯m B7(no3rd)

know, she would - n't say. I said

Em D C5 B5 Am6 D7 G5

some - thing wrong, now I long for yes - ter - day.

Verse

G5 F♯m B7(no3rd) Em Em/D

3., 4. Yes - ter - day, love was such an eas - y game to play,

Cmaj7 D7 G5 G5/F♯ Em7 A

now I need a place to hide a - way, Oh, I be - lieve in

Outro

C5 G5 G5 A7/G C5 G5

yes - ter - day. Mm.

RHYTHM TAB LEGEND

Rhythm Tab is a form of notation that adds rhythmic values to the traditional tab staff.

TABLATURE graphically represents the guitar fingerboard. Each horizontal line represents a string, and each number represents a fret. Rhythmic values are shown using ovals, stems, and dots.

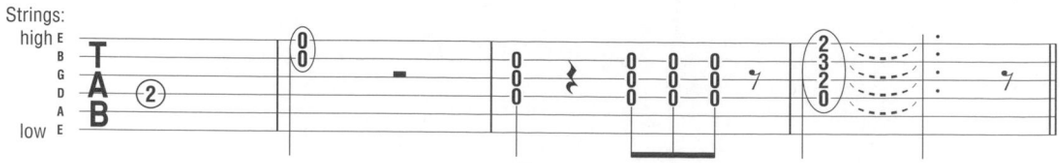

4th string, 2nd fret, played as a whole note

1st & 2nd strings open, played together as half notes

An open G chord, played as a quarter note and eighth notes

An open D chord, played and held for 3½ beats

Definitions for Special Guitar Notation

HALF-STEP BEND: Strike the note and bend up 1/2 step.

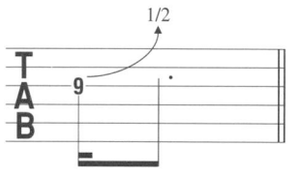

WHOLE-STEP BEND: Strike the note and bend up one step.

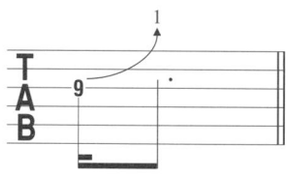

GRACE NOTE BEND: Strike the note and immediately bend up as indicated.

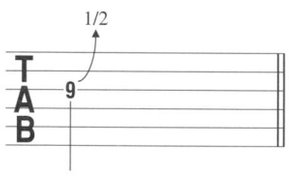

SLIGHT (MICROTONE) BEND: Strike the note and bend up 1/4 step.

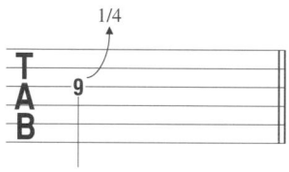

BEND AND RELEASE: Strike the note and bend up as indicated, then release back to the original note. Only the first note is struck.

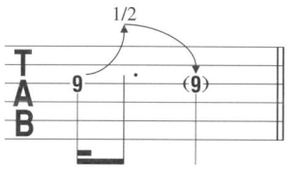

PRE-BEND: Bend the note as indicated, then strike it.

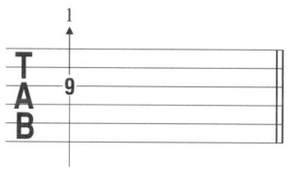

PRE-BEND AND RELEASE: Bend the note as indicated. Strike it and release the bend back to the original note.

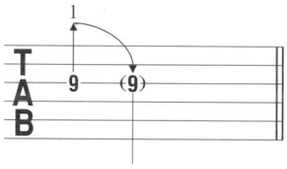

UNISON BEND: Strike the two notes simultaneously and bend the lower note up to the pitch of the higher.

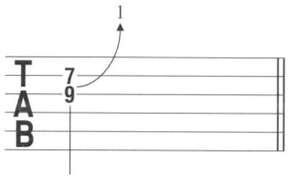

HOLD BEND: While sustaining bent note, strike note on different string.

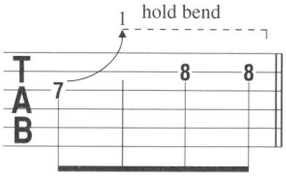

VIBRATO: The string is vibrated by rapidly bending and releasing the note with the fretting hand.

WIDE VIBRATO: The pitch is varied to a greater degree by vibrating with the fretting hand.

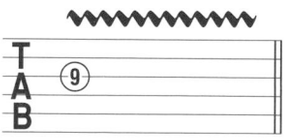

HAMMER-ON: Strike the first (lower) note with one finger, then sound the higher note (on the same string) with another finger by fretting it without picking.

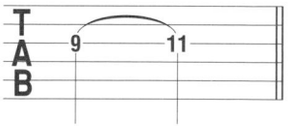

PULL-OFF: Place both fingers on the notes to be sounded. Strike the first note and without picking, pull the finger off to sound the second (lower) note.

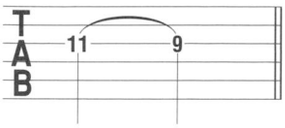

HAMMER FROM NOWHERE: Sound note(s) by hammering with fret hand finger only.

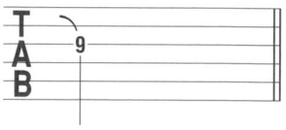

GRACE NOTE SLUR: Strike the note and immediately hammer-on (or pull-off) as indicated.

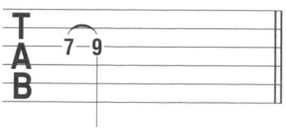

GRACE NOTE SLUR (CLUSTER): Strike the notes and immediately hammer-on (or pull-off) as indicated.

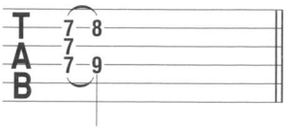

LEGATO SLIDE: Strike the first note and then slide the same fret-hand finger up or down to the second note. The second note is not struck.

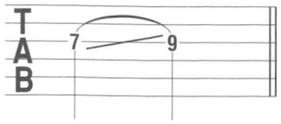

SHIFT SLIDE: Same as legato slide, except the second note is struck.

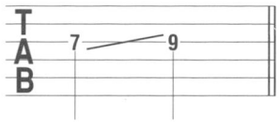

TRILL: Very rapidly alternate between the notes indicated by continuously hammering on and pulling off.

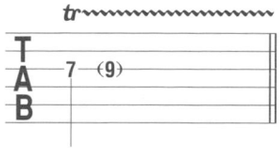

TAPPING: Hammer ("tap") the fret indicated with the pick-hand index or middle finger and pull off to the note fretted by the fret hand.

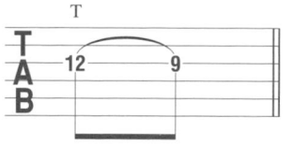

NATURAL HARMONIC: Strike the note while the fret-hand lightly touches the string directly over the fret indicated.

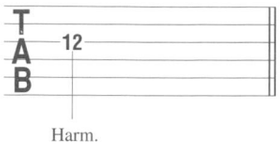

PINCH HARMONIC: The note is fretted normally and a harmonic is produced by adding the edge of the thumb or the tip of the index finger of the pick hand to the normal pick attack.

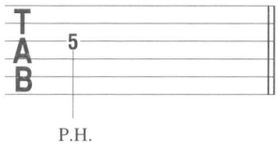

HARP HARMONIC: The note is fretted normally and a harmonic is produced by gently resting the pick hand's index finger directly above the indicated fret (in parentheses) while the pick hand's thumb or pick assists by plucking the appropriate string.

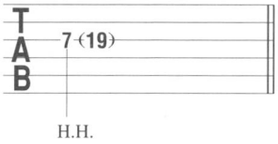

PICK SCRAPE: The edge of the pick is rubbed down (or up) the string, producing a scratchy sound.

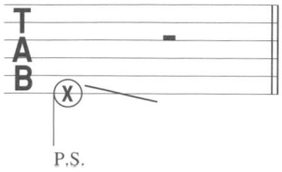

MUFFLED STRINGS: A percussive sound is produced by laying the fret hand across the string(s) without depressing, and striking them with the pick hand.

PALM MUTING: The note is partially muted by the pick hand lightly touching the string(s) just before the bridge.

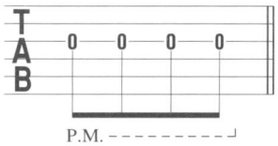

RAKE: Drag the pick across the strings indicated with a single motion.

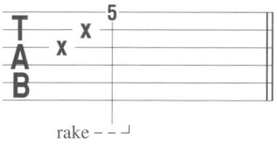

TREMOLO PICKING: The note is picked as rapidly and continuously as possible.

ARPEGGIATE: Play the notes of the chord indicated by quickly rolling them from bottom to top.

VIBRATO BAR DIVE AND RETURN: The pitch of the note or chord is dropped a specified number of steps (in rhythm), then returned to the original pitch.

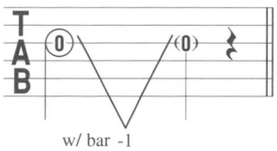

VIBRATO BAR SCOOP: Depress the bar just before striking the note, then quickly release the bar.

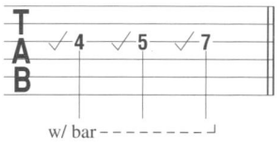

VIBRATO BAR DIP: Strike the note and then immediately drop a specified number of steps, then release back to the original pitch.

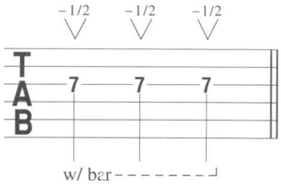

Additional Musical Definitions

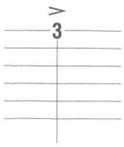

(accent) • Accentuate note (play it louder)

(staccato) • Play the note short

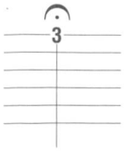

(fermata) • A hold or pause

• Downstroke

• Upstroke

• Repeat measures between signs

NOTE: Tablature numbers in parentheses are used when:

- The note is sustained, but a new articulation begins (such as a hammer-on, pull-off, slide, or bend), or
- A bend is released.

FIRST 50

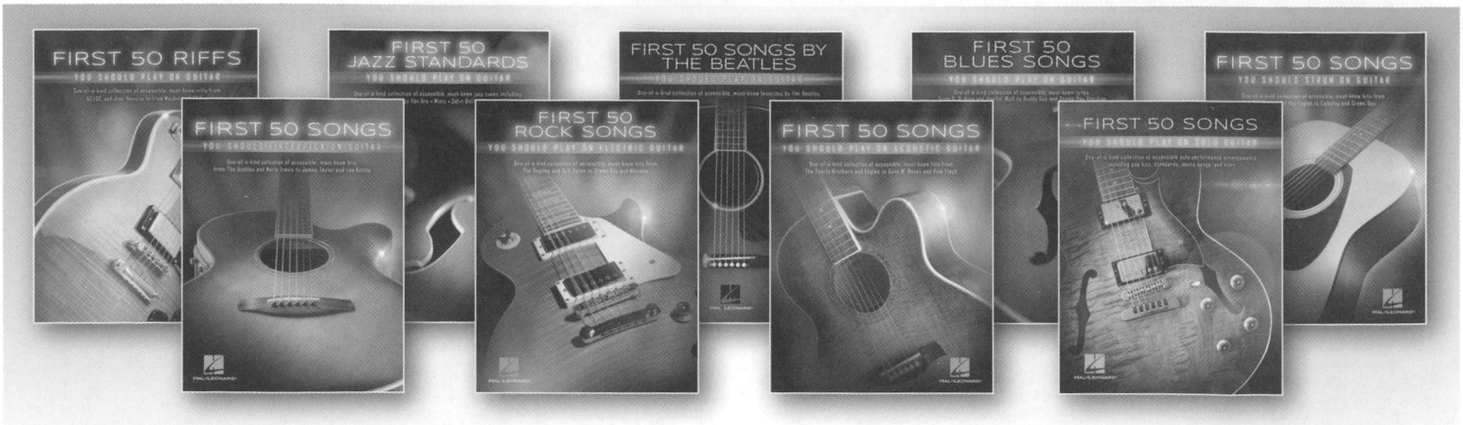

Books in the First 50 series contain easy to intermediate arrangements for must-know songs. Each arrangement is simple and streamlined, yet still captures the essence of the tune.

First 50 Baroque Pieces You Should Play on Guitar
Includes selections by Johann Sebastian Bach, Robert de Visée, Ernst Gottlieb Baron, Santiago de Murcia, Antonio Vivaldi, Sylvius Leopold Weiss, and more.
00322567 ..... $14.99

First 50 Bluegrass Solos You Should Play on Guitar
I Am a Man of Constant Sorrow • Long Journey Home • Molly and Tenbrooks • Old Joe Clark • Rocky Top • Salty Dog Blues • and more.
00298574 ..... $16.99

First 50 Blues Songs You Should Play on Guitar
All Your Love (I Miss Loving) • Bad to the Bone • Born Under a Bad Sign • Dust My Broom • Hoodoo Man Blues • Little Red Rooster • Love Struck Baby • Pride and Joy • Smoking Gun • Still Got the Blues • The Thrill Is Gone • You Shook Me • and more.
00235790 ..... $17.99

First 50 Blues Turnarounds You Should Play on Guitar
You'll learn cool turnarounds in the styles of these jazz legends: John Lee Hooker, Robert Johnson, Joe Pass, Jimmy Rogers, Hubert Sumlin, Stevie Ray Vaughan, T-Bone Walker, Muddy Waters, and more.
00277469 ..... $14.99

First 50 Chords You Should Play on Guitar
American Pie • Back in Black • Brown Eyed Girl • Landslide • Let It Be • Riptide • Summer of '69 • Take Me Home, Country Roads • Won't Get Fooled Again • You've Got a Friend • and more.
00300255 Guitar $12.99

First 50 Classical Pieces You Should Play on Guitar
Includes compositions by J.S. Bach, Augustin Barrios, Matteo Carcassi, Domenico Scarlatti, Fernando Sor, Francisco Tárrega, Robert de Visée, Antonio Vivaldi and many more.
00155414 ..... $16.99

First 50 Folk Songs You Should Play on Guitar
Amazing Grace • Down by the Riverside • Home on the Range • I've Been Working on the Railroad • Kumbaya • Man of Constant Sorrow • Oh! Susanna • This Little Light of Mine • When the Saints Go Marching In • The Yellow Rose of Texas • and more.
00235868 ..... $16.99

First 50 Guitar Duets You Should Play
Chopsticks • Clocks • Eleanor Rigby • Game of Thrones Theme • Hallelujah • Linus and Lucy (from *A Charlie Brown Christmas*) • Memory (from *Cats*) • Over the Rainbow (from *The Wizard of Oz*) • Star Wars (Main Theme) • What a Wonderful World • You Raise Me Up • and more.
00319706 ..... $14.99

First 50 Jazz Standards You Should Play on Guitar
All the Things You Are • Body and Soul • Don't Get Around Much Anymore • Fly Me to the Moon (In Other Words) • The Girl from Ipanema (Garota De Ipanema) • I Got Rhythm • Laura • Misty • Night and Day • Satin Summertime • When I Fall in Love • and more.
00198594 Solo Guitar $16.99

First 50 Kids' Songs You Should Play on Guitar
Do-Re-Mi • Hakuna Matata • Let It Go • My Favorite Things • Puff the Magic Dragon • Take Me Out to the Ball Game • Won't You Be My Neighbor? (It's a Beautiful Day in the Neighborhood) • and more.
00300500 ..... $15.99

First 50 Licks You Should Play on Guitar
Licks presented include the styles of legendary guitarists like Eric Clapton, Buddy Guy, Jimi Hendrix, B.B. King, Randy Rhoads, Carlos Santana, Stevie Ray Vaughan and many more.
00278875 Book/Online Audio $14.99

First 50 Riffs You Should Play on Guitar
All Right Now • Back in Black • Barracuda • Carry on Wayward Son • Crazy Train • La Grange • Layla • Seven Nation Army • Smoke on the Water • Sunday Bloody Sunday • Sunshine of Your Love • Sweet Home Alabama • Working Man • and more.
00277366 ..... $14.99

First 50 Rock Songs You Should Play on Electric Guitar
All Along the Watchtower • Beat It • Brown Eyed Girl • Cocaine • Detroit Rock City • Hallelujah • (I Can't Get No) Satisfaction • Oh, Pretty Woman • Pride and Joy • Seven Nation Army • Should I Stay or Should I Go • Smells like Teen Spirit • Smoke on the Water • When I Come Around • You Really Got Me • and more.
00131159 ..... $15.99

First 50 Songs by the Beatles You Should Play on Guitar
All You Need Is Love • Blackbird • Come Together • Eleanor Rigby • Hey Jude • I Want to Hold Your Hand • Let It Be • Ob-La-Di, Ob-La-Da • She Loves You • Twist and Shout • Yellow Submarine • Yesterday • and more.
00295323 ..... $19.99

First 50 Songs You Should Fingerpick on Guitar
Annie's Song • Blackbird • The Boxer • Classical Gas • Dust in the Wind • Fire and Rain • Greensleeves • Road Trippin' • Shape of My Heart • Tears in Heaven • Time in a Bottle • Vincent (Starry Starry Night) • and more.
00149269 ..... $16.99

First 50 Songs You Should Play on 12-String Guitar
California Dreamin' • Closer to the Heart • Free Fallin' • Give a Little Bit • Hotel California • Leaving on a Jet Plane • Life by the Drop • Over the Hills and Far Away • Solsbury Hill • Space Oddity • Wish You Were Here • You Wear It Well • and more.
00287559 ..... $15.99

First 50 Songs You Should Play on Acoustic Guitar
Against the Wind • Boulevard of Broken Dreams • Champagne Supernova • Every Rose Has Its Thorn • Fast Car • Free Fallin' • Layla • Let Her Go • Mean • One • Ring of Fire • Signs • Stairway to Heaven • Trouble • Wagon Wheel • Yellow • Yesterday • and more.
00131209 ..... $16.99

First 50 Songs You Should Play on Bass
Blister in the Sun • I Got You (I Feel Good) • Livin' on a Prayer • Low Rider • Money • Monkey Wrench • My Generation • Roxanne • Should I Stay or Should I Go • Uptown Funk • What's Going On • With or Without You • Yellow • and more.
00149189 ..... $16.99

First 50 Songs You Should Play on Solo Guitar
Africa • All of Me • Blue Skies • California Dreamin' • Change the World • Crazy • Dream a Little Dream of Me • Every Breath You Take • Hallelujah • Wonderful Tonight • Yesterday • You Raise Me Up • Your Song • and more.
00288843 ..... $17.99

First 50 Songs You Should Strum on Guitar
American Pie • Blowin' in the Wind • Daughter • Hey, Soul Sister • Home • I Will Wait • Losing My Religion • Mrs. Robinson • No Woman No Cry • Peaceful Easy Feeling • Rocky Mountain High • Sweet Caroline • Teardrops on My Guitar • Wonderful Tonight • and more.
00148996 Guitar $16.99

HAL•LEONARD®
www.halleonard.com
1022
014

Prices, contents and availability subject to change without notice.